ALSO BY LOUIS AUCHINCLOSS

FICTION

The Indifferent Children
The Injustice Collectors
Sybil
A Law for the Lion
The Romantic Egoists
The Great World and Timothy Colt
Venus in Sparta
Pursuit of the Prodigal
The House of Five Talents
Portrait in Brownstone
Powers of Attorney
The Rector of Justin
The Embezzler
Tales of Manhattan
A World of Profit

Second Chance
I Come as a Thief
The Partners
The Winthrop Covenant
The Dark Lady
The Country Cousin
The House of the Prophet
The Cat and the King
Watchfires
Narcissa and Other Fables
Exit Lady Masham
The Book Class
Honorable Men
Diary of a Yuppie
Skinny Island

NONFICTION

Reflections of a Jacobite
Pioneers and Caretakers
Motiveless Malignity
Edith Wharton
Richelieu
A Writer's Capital

Reading Henry James
Life, Law and Letters
Persons of Consequence: Queen Victoria
and Her Circle
False Dawn: Women in the
Age of the Sun King

THE VANDERBILT ERA

PROFILES OF A GILDED AGE

LOUIS AUCHINCLOSS

COLLIER BOOKS

MACMILLAN PUBLISHING COMPANY

NEW YORK

Collier Books
Macmillan Publishing Company
866 Third Avenue, New York, NY 10022
Collier Macmillan Canada, Inc.

Library of Congress Cataloging-in-Publication Data
Auchincloss, Louis.
The Vanderbilt era: profiles of a gilded age/Louis Auchincloss.
—1st Collier Books ed.
p.   cm.
ISBN 0-02-030310-6
1. Vanderbilt family.   2. New York (N.Y.)—Biography.   3. United
States—Social life and customs—1865–1918.   4. New York (N.Y.)—
Intellectual life—19th century.   5. Upper classes—New York
(N.Y.)—Biography.   I. Title.
[CT274.V35A93   1990]
974.7′1041′0922—dc20
[B]   89-28892   CIP

Macmillan books are available at special discounts for bulk purchases for
sales promotions, premiums, fund-raising, or educational use.
For details, contact:

Special Sales Director
Macmillan Publishing Company
866 Third Avenue
New York, NY 10022

First Collier Books Edition 1990

10 9 8 7 6 5 4 3 2 1

Printed in the United States of America

For Charles Scribner III,
worthy descendant of the great commodore
and "only begetter of these insuing"
sketches

CONTENTS

CONTENTS

The Vanderbilt Era

Biltmore, Asheville, North Carolina—under construction.

THE ERA that I have chosen so to designate is the period in American social history, centered to a large extent in the City of New York, that occupied the last two decades of the nineteenth and the first of the twentieth century. It is an era closely related, of course, to the Mauve Decade, the Edwardian Age, the *belle époque,* terms which inevitably evoke elegant and extravagant ways of life. I do not suggest that members of the Vanderbilt family were responsible for the era, or that they deserve particular credit or even particular blame for it. I chose them because they were richer and more numerous than any of the other clans that dominated business in the decades that followed the Civil War, and because they made a greater splash with their money. It is my contention that it was that splash, combined with all the other splashes from the great new fortunes of the time, that gave its principal features to that age of gold and alloy, providing fuel for the engines that were to produce, amid a great deal of undoubted ugliness, the artistic productions of what has sometimes been called, for better or worse, the American Renaissance.

The new rich of New York in the 1880s were not an aristocracy, nor did they succeed one. America has never had a true aristocracy, unless the old planters of the antebellum South were one. An aristocracy must have its base in the ownership and cultivation of land. The tradesmen and moneylenders of cities, no matter how long established and no matter what their personal dignity or moral code, can never be other than a bourgeoisie, which is why it never takes one class of capitalists very long to amalgamate with another. The Vanderbilts, Oelriches, and Millses were soon enough accepted by the old Knickerbocker families of Manhattan and Brooklyn. There were, to be sure, some delays to be accepted, some snubs to be endured, some parties to be given where guests of honor failed to arrive or sent a false excuse, even some bad loans to be made, but in the not very long run the two groups, sharing the broad common denominator of the stock market, submerged their few differences in sensible merger. Did not Vanderbilt even sound like Van Rensselaer?

Nobody has described this process more vividly or with more insight than Edith Wharton in her two finest novels, *The Age of Innocence* and *The House of Mirth*. The first takes place in New York not long after the end of the Civil War. Society is still dominated by the old families, whose gentle naïveté and remoteness from the sweep of new events are mirrored in the novel's title. Newland Archer, the hero, lives with his widowed mother and sister, lapped in self-satisfied brownstone security, in a neighborhood of friends and cousins whom they have known all their lives. He practices law in a mild, leisurely way, writing wills for relatives; he feels he is "advanced" because he reads French novels and belongs to the Century Club, and he is contemplating marriage with his female counterpart, May Welland. The new rich are only a vague threat as yet, represented by the brilliant and flamboyant banker Julius Beaufort (modeled on the German-Jewish financier August Belmont), whose glib tongue, vast fortune, and marriage into an old family have brought him to a position of actual leadership. He is the first person to build a ballroom onto his house to be used only for dancing. Liberation comes to Newland in the form of his fiancée's cousin, the lovely and Europeanized Ellen, who has left her rich, titled beast of a husband, Count Olenski, to retreat to what she regards as the "unreal" but consoling Garden of Eden of her brownstone childhood. She opens up new worlds to Newland; she makes him understand that hitherto he has been only half alive. They fall in love and wish to go off together, but it is too late. For in the meantime he has married her cousin, and his dull but loving wife is pregnant. Now the reader will see with what force and efficiency that old, inert New York society could act to protect its own. It may have had neither the muscle nor the will to expel the "invader" Beaufort, but when it comes to adultery, all members, old and young, join forces in a silent but grimly effective drive to tighten Newland's domestic bonds and send poor Ellen packing back to Europe where she belongs.

The diary of George Templeton Strong, a New York lawyer and a contemporary and acquaintance of Edith Wharton's father, describes how in the late 1850s very much the same procedure was unleashed against a "bounder" who was trying to persuade the wife of a cousin of the diarist to run off with him. By the time Strong was through with him, this rash young man faced a line of slammed brownstone front doors as rigid and unyielding as the row of lowered horns that the musk oxen present to the threatening wolf.

The House of Mirth, published in 1905, deals with an approximately contemporary New York scene. More than thirty years have passed since Newland Archer was obliged to give up love for duty, and the social scene has drastically changed. The merger of the old and new forces is virtually complete, and up and down Fifth Avenue they attend the same parties. The Van Osburghs, who bring to mind the Vanderbilts, reign supreme, and if Mrs. Peniston, the rigid, conservative old aunt of the heroine, Lily Bart, still tends to raise her nose at some of the goings on, nobody much cares. It is hard now to tell which of the characters is "Knickerbocker" and which an "invader." Because Lily's bankrupt father was a brother of Mrs. Peniston, he must have been the former, but a hint of vulgarity in the brief description of her mother suggests that Lily herself was the fruit of merger. The Dorsets and Trenors strike me as second-generation "invaders," now confident of their position. The Wellington Brys, on the other hand, who have retained the secret services of Carrie Fisher to assist them in their climb, are obviously still on a lower rung of the social ladder, although the guests at the reception where Lily makes her last great impression in the *tableaux vivants* would seem to indicate that they were rising more rapidly than their agent believed. Sim Rosedale, a Jew and a too crudely passionate climber, would be beyond the pale were it not that his financial clout has made him feared by some of the husbands of the more socially secure.

As poor Lily, who is too fastidious to marry just for money and too worldly to marry just for love, finds herself dropping from rung to rung, she keeps meeting people on their way up who cut her at once when they recognize her downward trend, until she finally reaches the nadir of the demimonde where all hope is extinguished of any social advance. Yet even at this level there is a hint that foolish Freddy Van Osburgh may join her by making a misalliance with Lily's blond employer. But Freddy might one day make his way back, thanks to his fortune, even accompanied by his reputationless spouse. But of course there is no redemption for a woman who has let herself sink so far, even if, like Lily, she has retained her virginity.

But I must get back to the Vanderbilts, the Van Osburghs of Lily Bart's New York. *Was* there such a thing as a Vanderbilt? What exactly, in other words, is a family? Is it limited to descendants of the founder in the male line who share his surname? Social historians are apt to take this view, partly, I suspect, because it makes the assessment of characteristics simpler. If I wish to prove, as many such do, or certainly used to, that plutocratic families tend to peter out into decadence, it is neat to be able to contrast an alcoholic and spendthrift Reginald Vanderbilt with his industrious and sober grandsire, William Henry, or the seven-times-married minor journalist, Cornelius IV, with the hale old commodore. But if I look further up the multitudinous branches of the Vanderbilt family tree, and if I choose from distaff ones, I can with equal neatness refute the theory by citing William A. M. Burden, who not only strikingly resembled his great-grandfather William Henry, but showed all the latter's genius in converting his five talents into ten, served his nation as an able and distinguished ambassador to Belgium, and put together a famous art collection. Or Douglas Burden, the explorer and naturalist? Or, even without abandoning the male line, Harold Vanderbilt, the inventor of contract bridge, which occupies more of the time of more of our citizens than anyone would care to admit? I could go on and on.

I suppose the idea of a family constituting a generic unit, even over a period of many generations, sprang from the examples of certain royal families whose constant intermarriages preserved a consanguineous resemblance. The "Habsburg lip" or the "Bourbon nose" continued from age to age where cousins always married cousins. Louis XV was descended from Henry of Navarre through four of the latter's legitimate children and one of his bastards. Louis XIV and his Spanish consort were double first cousins. In the House of Austria an uncle could marry his own niece with an easily obtained papal dispensation.

Of course in early communities where there was little traveling and only a small number of families in each social class, something of the same nature might obtain. I know that in the village of Stonington in Connecticut, whose genealogical records were carefully kept, I can find the same couple over and over in my own line of ascent. But it's all very far back. Intermarriages of close kin are rare today. There are living many hundreds of Commodore Vanderbilt's descendants, all perfectly verifiable and identifiable (though only a scant few with the family surname), and I have been able to find only one instance of intermarriage among them. I doubt, furthermore, that that young couple were even aware they were related when they met. Modern society hardly considers third and fourth cousins kin.

Some years ago Vanderbilt University, founded with a grant from the commodore (and not a very large one, even by the humbler standards of that day), conceived of the plan of compiling a book of all of his descendants and inviting the living to attend a reunion in Nashville. It proved a great success, both socially and as a fund-raiser, for although few of the guests were still endowed with any great portion of the original fortune, many had made, married, or inherited other fortunes, and all were intrigued by the reassembling of the clan.

Except of course it wasn't really a clan at all; that is just the point I am trying to make. After a certain time any man's descendants, in different lines, have ceased to bear any real relation to one another. That is why I have limited the "Vanderbilts" in these essays to the first three generations after the commodore. And even that may be justified only by the continuance of the family looks longer than in other clans owing to the fact that the commodore and his first wife, Sophia Johnson, mother of his twelve children, were first cousins.

The society created from 1880 to 1910 by the daughters-in-law of William Henry Vanderbilt, Alice and Alva, and by Mrs. William Astor, Mrs. Ogden Mills, Mrs. Paran Stevens, Mrs. Stuyvesant Fish, and a great many other hard-working ladies (Alva Vanderbilt claimed there was no tougher job than a society leader's) was basically flawed in that it had no real relation to society in the larger sense of the word. It had nothing to do with the political structure of the nation or any of its states; its leaders were not even nominal peers—their imagined "rank," such as it was, had no connection with any sovereign, court, or recognized fountain of honors. This is illustrated by a silly story told of Mrs. Cornelius Vanderbilt III (the frequently fatuous "Grace"), who allegedly protested, when given an inferior table at a London restaurant, that in her native land she took a position somewhat analogous to that of "your princess of Wales." "Oh?" the headwaiter is supposed to have responded. "And who, pray, is your sovereign?"

Secondly, the world whose essence was supposed to be containable within the four walls of Mrs. Astor's ballroom had little to do with the arts and letters, except insofar as—and this was to become very important—it provided patrons and collectors. It did not, at least in its early stages, cultivate social relations with writers and painters. The hostesses of Fifth Avenue, like Queen Victoria herself, had little wish to be made uncomfortable by intellectuals chattering about books they hadn't read or pictures they didn't understand. It was a society where the men cared mostly for business and sport, and the women for dress and parties. The same might have been said of the older Knickerbocker society with which it had merged, but the activities of the latter had been conducted on too modest a scale to be much noted by the world at large.

The social activities of the Vanderbilt era, on the other hand, were of a dimension to make headlines in the newspapers of the day and to have found their way into serious historical and sociological studies. Fifth Avenue was turned into a kind of historical pageant of castles and palaces. Even so serious a writer as Willa Cather, and one devoted to the wide-open spaces of her native Nebraska, found a favorite diversion, when she moved to New York, in riding up that fantastic boulevard on the open top of a bus and taking in the view of the royal replicas of a transplanted Loire Valley, already in her day doomed to demolition.

I suppose it is obvious that a society which erected such residences would find a fitting outlet for its romantic imagination in the fancy-dress ball. For what did they dress up as? Sometimes literary characters, it is true, sometimes even comic ones, but the prevailing favorites were invariably royalties or courtiers: Mary, Queen of Scots; Marie Antoinette; Madame du Barry; Cardinal Richelieu. The great imported portals of their mansions, which opened in the daytime to admit gentlemen with derby hats and ladies in veils with muffs, could at night usher into brilliantly lit interiors a host of guests garbed as splendidly as any those doors had known of yore.

But here I must pause; I must be fair. Just as what used to be called "vulgar Americanisms," now spread over the globe to make it one world of high-rises, parking lots, and rock music, compel the recognition by our neighbors, however reluctant, that we have been the pioneers of "modernism" and not the proselytizers of a culture specifically indigenous, so should the extravagances of the Vanderbilt era be redefined as simply the local aspect of an international fever. I have recently examined an illustrated book on the famous costume ball given in 1902 by the duke and duchess of Devonshire to celebrate the accession of Edward VII. There I recognized all the same silly poses in all the same elaborately extravagant costumes that I had seen in the New York albums of the same period, but here the difference was that it was noblemen and royalties who dressed up as earlier noblemen and royalties. And it struck me that it seemed no more indigenous, no more fitting to the period than the W. K. Vanderbilt ball of 1883 or the Bradley Martins' of 1896. Indeed, it seemed almost less so, as if those strutting creatures, arrayed in the trappings of a more picturesque past, were proclaiming with a kind of mad folly that they were indeed anachronisms, that their day was done. And wasn't it? A few more years would sweep most of it away, leaving the royal family itself to survive only as a species of venerated soap opera for the delectation of the masses.

But I have dwelt enough on parties. The Gilded Age itself, as opposed to the gilded persons in it, was filled with artists and thinkers. In these essays I have not included the radicals who wished to overturn it, or the countless sensible people who lived entirely apart from it, but rather some of those, along with the Vanderbilts themselves, who entertained it, decorated it, built and sculpted for it, painted it, wrote about it, and even, like the Adams brothers, viewed it from the inside with a passionate scorn, which became in itself a kind of art.

If Henry James might be considered a refugee from the Vanderbilt era, he was certainly a penetrating observer of it. The winter that he spent in New York City after the end of the Civil War was quite enough to convince him that a society was in the making where money and business would be the only acceptable interests for the conventionally successful male. He divined the new distinction, hardly a feature of the old Knickerbocker society, between downtown and uptown. The men, the "real" men, went downtown, leaving Henry to write in his rented uptown room in a brownstone daytime domain of women. There were, of course, men—or should we say "males"—left north of Canal Street, and they performed no doubt useful tasks, such as keeping shops and designing clothes and decorating houses, even, perhaps, writing novels, but their accomplishments had little to do with the high events of the stock market or the law courts. Their function was to amuse the women and keep them from being too jealous, not only of the long hours their mates devoted to Mammon, but of the almost exclusive devotion they offered to that deity. The nonworking man uptown was symbolized by the epicene figure of the cotillion leader—Ward McAllister.

James settled in England, where, having no "rank," a foreigner was acceptable to any class with which he chose to associate himself, and he was thus able to avoid the brambles of the rigid British hierarchical system. One wonders if, born in England of the same bourgeois origin as the Jameses of Albany, he might have cast his eyes westward to horizons of less crushing snobbishness. But on either side of the Atlantic he would have been an equally great artist and an equally acute observer. When he revisited America in 1903, after an uninterrupted absence of twenty years, the gained perspective was to assist him in writing one of his greatest books and probably the most incisive study of the United States since Tocqueville's.

It has taken *The American Scene,* published in 1905, a long time to be recognized as the remarkable assessment of American life that it is. The style, which is the ultimately splendid one of James's so-called major phase, is, alas, too often "caviar to the general," and some of his observations were seized upon by hostile critics as the frettings of an old expatriate bachelor who could find culture and comfort only in aristocratic European settings. Examples of this were his scorn of what he deemed the falsely democratic habit of calling a laundress a "washerlady," his condemnation of Florida because he couldn't get a snack in a first-class hotel after midnight, and his query, when a black porter placed on his lap the attaché case that had been standing in a muddy street, if *this* were the service for which the old planters had fought and bled. But aside from a few such grumblings his observations were uncannily accurate.

He saw that the cities were doomed to build themselves over every generation and that no new skyscraper was any safer than a condemned landmark. The newest and proudest construction, he noted, had nonetheless a haunted look—it knew its days were already numbered. He saw that our native heritage of seemingly unbounded forests and meadows was already threatened by planless development, and in the English edition he put in the mouth of an American Indian a bitter denunciation of what was going on. He saw the preemptive role that moneymaking was playing and continued to doubt that there would have been any real place for him in his native land. And he had the sharpness to understand that the new institution of the country club, long considered a bastion of exclusiveness, was really, at least by European standards, a democratic body, as the criterion for membership was not family or position but simply wealth, however acquired.

His dismay at what he saw endowed his own American past with a charm he had not hitherto appreciated, and he found this particularly so in Newport. He remembered with a tense nostalgia the simple little watering place it had been with its lovely sea air and enchanting half-hidden bays. But now the great white palaces along the Cliff Walk, huddled senselessly together as if they were afraid to venture down Bellevue Avenue alone, struck him as appallingly out of tune, not only with the natural scene but with any human culture that paid the scantest attention to laws of restraint and balance. He likened the old Newport of his childhood, in a famous simile, to a little white hand which had been suddenly crammed with gold.

He might have intended this image as the epitaph of the Vanderbilt era. But to that era, can I not also argue, belong, at least to some extent, the richly phrased pages of *The American Scene* itself, as well as the characters and stories of those golden works of fiction, *The Wings of the Dove* and *The Golden Bowl*?

The Commodore

Commodore Cornelius Vanderbilt by Eastman Johnson.
MUSEUM OF THE CITY OF NEW YORK

HIS CHARACTER is a hard one to catch. The recorded memories of him run to black and white. There are no subtleties, few ambiguities.

Charles Francis Adams's summary in 1913 of nineteenth-century capitalists is well known: "I have known, and known tolerably well, a good many 'successful' men—'big' financially—men famous during the last half century, and a less interesting crowd I do not care to encounter. Not one that I have ever known would I care to meet again, either in this world or the next; nor is one of them associated in my mind with the idea of humor, thought or refinement. A set of mere money-makers and traders, they were essentially unattractive and uninteresting."

Cornelius Vanderbilt belongs to a slightly earlier era; Adams did not know him. But he wrote about him, and nothing that he wrote suggests that he would have found in him an exception to his general rule. Yet certainly Vanderbilt strikes one as the very opposite of the dry, etiolated, black-garbed accumulator evoked by the name of Gould, whom Adams detested and of whom Vanderbilt himself said, "No man can have such countenance as his and still be honest." Indeed, appearance to the commodore may have had something to do with his concept of honesty. He himself looked like a conqueror. No capitalist but the first J. P. Morgan even approached him in this.

He was a tall, thin six feet one, a great height for a man born in the eighteenth century (1794) to have attained. He had a clear complexion, ruddy cheeks, a large bold head, a strong nose, square jaw, a high, confidence-inspiring brow, and thick, long gray hair which turned magnificently white. If he gave his mornings to business, he was never a grind. In the afternoons, at least in his later years, he drove out with his trotters, racing anyone encountered along the road who would accept the challenge, and was not averse to dashing across a grade crossing before a charging locomotive. At night he drank whiskey and played whist with his cronies.

In 1851, finding that it was not feasible to build a canal across Nicaragua, Vanderbilt, still in his steamship period, devised a plan to run his vessels from New York to San Juan del Norte, take his passengers thence by riverboat up the San Juan River to San Carlos, transfer them to a lake steamer which would ferry them across Lake Nicaragua to Virgin Bay, and there put them on a train to carry them the twelve miles to the Pacific and to a Vanderbilt steamer bound for San Francisco. When it was pointed out to him that no steamer could endure the first part of the trans-isthmian passage through the rapids of the San Juan River, Vanderbilt, visiting the site, took the wheel of the steamer himself, tied down the safety valve, and bounced and scraped the vessel over rocks and through churning rapids up the 119 miles to San Carlos.

Five years later, when he was sixty, he was reputed to have beaten almost senseless a champion pugilist who, in a New York political riot, had grabbed the reins of his horse to compel him to dismount. And at sixty-seven, during the Civil War, he made the offer to President Lincoln to take the wheel of his steamship *Vanderbilt* and hunt down the Confederate ironclad *Merrimac* to "strike her amidships and sink her." And he actually took the vessel to the mouth of the James River in search of his opponent, which never appeared.

So far the man of force, without apparent peer. But what about the egotist? For here too he seems to have been a nonpareil. He was always being painted or sculpted, and surely no man of his age could have had more ships named for him. Ernest Plassman's giant frock-coated statue, which now adorns the southern façade of Grand Central Station, gazing serenely down the ramp to lower Park Avenue, was originally situated above the gate of Saint John's Park Freight Station, where it constituted the centerpiece for a gigantic bas-relief, measuring more than three thousand square feet and illustrating the commodore's career. A figure of Neptune blessed the steamer *Vanderbilt*; one of Liberty paid tribute to the locomotive *C. Vanderbilt* with its train of cars.

16

"These be thy gods, O Israel!" George Templeton Strong recorded bitterly in his journal after the unveiling in 1869, appending the sour hope that the bas-relief had not been paid for by the community but by "Vanderbilt's jackals and subordinates." Mayor Oakey Hall expressed a different sentiment: "Stand there, familiar image of an honored man! Stand there and tell whose industry has been crowned by wealth that the honors of life and the praise of future generations follow those, and those only, who make the world better for those living it."

One wonders that any audience could have tolerated such unctuous flattery as Hall's, but it must be recalled that Vanderbilt's official biographer, W. A. Croffut, unblushingly applied the phrase "puffed with divine greed" to his subject and did not hesitate to opine that "the desire to own property is the chief difference between the savage and the enlightened man." It was an era that did not shrink from fatuity and perhaps reached its culmination (if not its finale) with a statement in 1901 by William Lawrence, Episcopal bishop of Massachusetts: "Material prosperity is helping to make the national character sweeter, more joyous, more unselfish, more Christlike."

So much for Vanderbilt's forcefulness. I have said the record is black and white. What about the black? In response to those who claim that Vanderbilt had a great role in developing necessary transportation for a growing nation, it should be stated that for years he idled all the vessels on his East-to-West-Coast Nicaraguan route in response to heavy bribes from the owners of the rival Panamanian passage. And if he showed a fine patriotic spirit in offering to sink the *Merrimac,* it is equally true that the vessels that he chartered to the U.S. Navy for the expedition to New Orleans turned out to be rotten and unfit for ocean duty.

The contrast between heorism and meanness is constantly baffling in the study of his long career. The man who was willing to kindle a small civil war in Nicaragua against such unprincipled adventurers as the shippers Cornelius Garrison and Charles Morgan and the wild Central American political fanatic William Walker; the man who, after seventy, had the foresight and energy to alter his main interest from steamships to railroads, build the empire of the New York Central lines, and put together the largest fortune in the world; the man who could bust a corrupt city council and a vicious state legislature by his genius at cornering stock, was also the man who knew better than any other how to buy judges and lawmakers and how to shove off on the public the cheapest and tawdriest services to enhance his profits.

But wasn't that the way things were done? Testifying before a state railway commission he said: "I stated awhile ago that I for one will never go to a court of law when I have the power in my own hands to see myself right. Let the other parties go to law if they will, but by *** [deleted expletive], I think I know what the law is; I have had enough of it." And indeed he had, from his earliest days as an uneducated lad, piloting his own boat in the tough New York waterfront, where a ramming prow and a ready fist were better than any lawyer, to his later career in the mart of unregulated businesses where inspectors, judges, and legislators were frankly for sale. Vanderbilt had the reputation for a kind of integrity: in deals over competition and the refraining therefrom he would stay bought. And he was loyal to his own.

His defense by Henry Clews in *Fifty Years in Wall Street* sadly illuminates the times. Clews states positively that "everyone" who knew Vanderbilt and his lifelong enemy-crony, Daniel Drew, was of the opinion that with a fair or liberal education neither would have cut a prominent figure as a financier. Clews even doubts if they would have been capable, given their peculiar predilections, of receiving a college education. Could any teacher, he asks, have convinced the commodore that there was anything wrong with his expression "Never tell nobody what yer goin' to do till you do it" or Drew that "shares" were not "sheers"?

In other words, education, or even a mild cultivation, was a hindrance in the wilderness of Wall Street. And Clews's example of a rare act of generosity on Vanderbilt's part is significant. Possessed of what we would call an "insider's" knowledge that Central was about to declare an eighty-percent dividend, the commodore, bethinking himself of the plight of an old and bankrupt crony, tipped off another crony under condition that the tippee would split his profits with their needy pal. This "generosity," without cost to himself, would have been a criminal act today.

The era's different moral climate in business did not extend to a man's private life. Indeed, there it may have been higher than our own, and Vanderbilt fell very short of contemporary standards. When his first wife (and first cousin), Sophia Johnson Vanderbilt, mother of his twelve children, refused to move from Staten Island, which suited her simpler tastes, to his new and much grander residence on Washington Place in Manhattan, he had her placed in an asylum until she changed her mind. He did the same with his epileptic son, Cornelius Jeremiah, when the latter became a constant gambler and a troublesome drunk. He was reputed to have cared little for his many daughters and to have declined to save even a favored grandson from bankruptcy. His son, William Henry, to whom he ultimately bequeathed his empire, he treated for years with undisguised contempt, calling him "good for nothing," "beetlehead," and "blatherskite," recognizing and promoting him only when he proved at last that he had an aptitude for gainful trade. He gave only a tiny percentage of his fortune to charity, including the unexampled million-dollar endowment to an eponymous university, and this largely under the prodding of a much younger second wife on whom, in his old age, he had become in part dependent. On his deathbed he hurled hot-water bottles at his doctors and bellowed profanities that they were "old grannies" and "stupid fools." And finally, in bequeathing William Henry almost ninety percent of his estate, he demonstrated a favoritism that was virtually an expression of contempt for his other nine surviving children.

In the will fight that followed (ultimately settled with relatively minor concessions by the residuary legatee), Jeremiah S. Black, counsel for the contestants, a former chief justice of Pennsylvania and the kind of stagey orator, complete with booming tones and shaggy eyebrows, so popular in courts of that day, endeavored to persuade the surrogate that the decedent's cupidity amounted to a kind of madness:

He had one faculty that was preternaturally enlarged, and that was for accumulating property. It was so enlarged that it dwarfed every other moral sentiment and every intellectual power. Sanity depends upon the balance that has been preserved between the different intellectual faculties and moral sentiments so that all of them bear their proper proportions to one another. Suppose a man's liver to be enlarged beyond what it ought to be, is that man a healthy man? Cornelius Vanderbilt's bump of acquisitiveness, as a phrenologist would call it, was in a chronic state of inflammation all the time. It grew wonderfully. And he cultivated it, and under his cultivation all the intellectual faculties that ministered to the gratification of that passion at the expense of everything else. Morally and intellectually his mind was a howling wilderness.

But the surrogate concluded that the testimony showed the testator to have been a man of "very vigorous mind and strong nature, but lacking the amenities of education and culture and a delicate respect for the opinions of his fellow men."

We, too, can rebut some of the other accusations, at least by speculation. Who knows that Sophia may not have been suffering from some deep depression that justified her being relegated for a time to a mental institution? And Cornelius Jeremiah was probably irredeemable. I like the commodore's remark after one of the latter's more egregious defalcations: "I'd give a hundred dollars not to have named him Cornelius." Not a hundred thousand or even a thousand: the commodore knew the value of money. As for the daughters, I suspect they were not a very loving lot. Certainly Mrs. Labau was violently spiteful in the will case. They may have had little cause to love their father, but he did give them money, not much, to be sure, in view of what he had, but enough for them to live well by the standards of the day. And we should remember that the commodore was a great believer in people learning to look after themselves and had even, as a young man, been something of a socialist, going so far as to assert the view that no man should be allowed to have more than twenty thousand dollars.

The only two people the commodore seems to have loved were his mother, Phoebe, and his son George. The one portrait we have of Phoebe shows her as an old woman in a mob cap, draped in a shawl, with a man's face, comically like her son's, under the frills, a very strong nose and chin, and eyes and lips expressing a shrewd but humorous appraisal of what she sees. She supplied the commodore with strength and encouragement during much of his life. She was too old to go with him on the European cruise of the *North Star,* but the great yacht saluted her as it passed her home on Staten Island. When she died he consulted spiritualists to get in touch with her. He also used them for market tips.

George was more like an only than a favorite child. Handsome as the father whom he much resembled, strong (he could lift nine hundred pounds), and independently minded, he was the son the commodore had dreamed of. No objection was offered when he preferred a military career to a business one. He went to West Point and then served in the Civil War, where he contracted the malarial fever of which he died at twenty-five. The distracted commodore went back to his mediums and for the rest of his days tried to communicate with George.

I suspect that the commodore may have suffered more than his associates thought from his lack of cultivation, particularly as his constantly increasing preeminence exposed him to the public gaze. At times he would face this with defiance, perhaps even exaggerating his coarseness to throw in the faces of critics the bald fact that his uneducated brain had brought its owner the largest fortune of all. Would Greek or Latin have done that? It was a relief for him, no doubt, to surround himself with dependents and cronies where he could drink and cuss at will. But the hotel lobby in Saratoga and the tavern life of New York were in sharp contrast to daytime hours in the small bare chamber in Bowling Green where he worked, aided by a single secretary, at a table with one drawer containing a box of cigars. The files of his railroad enterprises were essentially in his mind.

There were times, particularly in the later years, when he seemed to be trying to show a better face to the world. In 1851 he took his great private steamer, the *North Star*—soon to be converted to a passenger ship as had always been his prudent plan—to visit the capitals of Europe on a family cruise. The dining saloon, in which foreign dignitaries would be entertained, had bulkheads of ligneous marble with panels of Neapolitan granite and an overhead covered with medallion paintings of such worthies in American history as Columbus, Washington, Clay, and Webster. On board were twenty Vanderbilts and consorts, a doctor, and a minister, the Reverend John O. Choules, who wrote an amusing account of the journey.

Choules found his host's manners something of a surprise: "Yet till I entered upon this voyage I did not adequately appreciate his knowledge of men, his fine tact, his intuitive perception of the fitting, and his dignified self-control; and I felt glad that such a man, self-made as he is, should be seen by the accidental sons of nobility and fortune in the Old World."

While it is true that Choules's unguarded remark to a reporter at the end of the cruise that "the commodore did the swearing and I did the preaching, so we never disagreed," might seem to modify the above, there are glimpses throughout the book of the tycoon trying with some earnestness to adapt himself becomingly to novel situations.

At a dinner party given in his honor by the mayor of Southampton, where the recorded speeches run to thirty pages of Choules's text, the commodore limited himself to a mere dozen courteous lines and then asked his son-in-law, Horace Clark, to speak for him. In Florence he was sculpted by Hiram Powers, who was delighted with his subject's head and figure. Vanderbilt was "charmed" with the sculptor's conversation and work, particularly admiring his "De Soto Taking Possession of the Mississippi Country," commissioned for the rotunda of the Capitol in Washington. As a connoisseur of horse flesh, he told Powers, he deemed the conquistador's steed the finest he had seen. But there were moments, as on any long trip, when the old temper was seen. Angered in Leghorn by a delay caused by a health officer, he impatiently ordered his captain to bypass Rome and go on to Naples, ignoring the cruel disappointment of those passengers to whom a visit to the Eternal City had been the main attraction of the trip.

That the commodore was not a vindictive man, that he took his revenge when he deemed it justified and then closed the books, is illustrated by his long relationship with Daniel Drew. Drew was a type that couldn't have existed in any country but America or in any era but the middle of the last century: the timid, quavering, psalm-singing, prudish, revivalist fanatic who felt entirely at liberty to cheat and steal at will and who lived for the excitement of the game of doing so. To have told him that a business corporation had any function but to be looted by its managers and shareholders would have been like telling a shark to spit out a tuna. When he was caught in a bad deal, he would use lies, dirty tricks, tearful pleas of innocence and poverty—anything to avoid paying a penny that he owed. His only faintly attractive quality was his total lack of interest in anything money could buy, either in worldly possessions or social position. Manipulating securities provided in itself all the joy he knew.

If such a man was capable of affection, he probably liked the commodore. And Vanderbilt seems to have enjoyed the company of this ugly little man, though outside the stock market they hadn't a single interest in common. Vanderbilt did not resent Drew's trying to ruin him; Drew tried to ruin everyone: it was what he was. Again and again Vanderbilt would disarm him with a brilliant cornering of railroad stock, and then, so to speak, toss him back his weapon for another bout. He, too, liked dangerous games, but he only undertook them when he knew he could win. And besides, did he and Drew not share the bond of a paucity of education?

Clifford Browder in his life of Drew gives an amusing account of how Frances ("Frank") Crawford Vanderbilt, the hearty and cheerful young cousin whom Sophia's widower had married and who was determined to bring the aging spouse whom she unaccountably adored nearer to God, entered into an alliance with Drew to induce the commodore to fund the establishment of a new church.

With great delicacy Frank Vanderbilt also managed to introduce her husband to her pastor, the Rev. Charles F. Deems, who became a frequent guest in the house and in time a good friend of the commodore. Exercising the greatest tact, Deems, Mrs. Vanderbilt and Drew conspired to interest the tightfisted Vanderbilt in Deems's project to establish a church of his own in the city, serving the needs of the out-of-town visitors. By June 1870 they had brought the old man around. He gave Deems fifty thousand dollars with which the minister bought a vacant church on Mercer Street that he opened in October of that year as the Church of the Strangers. Drew was one of the many prominent vice-presidents of its organizing committee. Thereafter, to the novelty of Cornelius Vanderbilt, the founder of a church, succeeded the near-miracle of Cornelius Vanderbilt, the worshiper. On February 19, 1871, Drew and the commodore appeared together in a pew in Deems's church; a sight so memorable that Deems recorded it in his private journal. To Uncle Daniel the event must have brought deep satisfaction; it was high time the old rat got religion!

Drew, like England, seems to have lost all battles but the last one. Certainly, seven years later, when the commodore lay dying in great agony with many physical malfunctions, the church was present in his chamber and hymns were sung by the assembled family in which the expiring ancestor joined. And when Deems approached the bedside, Vanderbilt told him, with tears in his eyes, "Doctor, I sent to you to tell you how I love you."

It must have been like a scene in an old farce, with the heirs hypocritically weeping over the death of the miser. The real tears would come when the will was read.

WILLIAM HENRY

The William H. Vanderbilt family by Seymour Guy.
From left to right: William Henry, Frederick,
Maria Kissam Vanderbilt, George (*seated*), Florence, William K.,
Lila (*seated*), Margaret Shepard (*holding fan*), Elliott Shepard,
Emily Sloane, Alice Vanderbilt (*seated*), W. D. Sloane,
Cornelius II, and two servants in the background.

I T TOOK William Henry Vanderbilt a long time to become his father's acknowledged heir. Until he was approaching middle age the latter had regarded him as unlikely material for the management of either ships or rails and consigned him to a farm on Staten Island. The commodore was willing to use his daughters' husbands from time to time in his business transactions, but he had strong dynastic views, and nobody to his way of thinking could be a "real" Vanderbilt but a son or son's son. Had George lived there is little question that, even as an army officer, he would have been involved in the control of the empire, but George was tragically dead, and Cornelius Jeremiah was hopeless. There was really no one to turn to but William unless the commodore could live long enough to hand things over to William's sons. Fortunately William was showing unmistakable signs of developing the "divine greed." Not only did he make an astonishingly good thing of the meager farm, but when he was named receiver of a small, bust thirteen-mile railway in Staten Island, he turned the company around and made its stock a profitable investment. William was sent to Manhattan to get his training under Daniel Drew! Yet it was probably a good idea. The man who could deal with Drew could deal with anyone.

So well did the two get on that Drew named his last-born child for William. The younger Vanderbilt seemed to have a genius for accommodation. Yet there is something distasteful in the picture of this homely, stout, phlegmatic man, with his small pig eyes and long, flowing side whiskers, bearing without a murmur the insults of his irascible sire and ending up with the whole fortune in his pocket. It was even said that he procured his young cousin, Frank Crawford, to be his father's second wife, figuring that she might contain the old man's lust and be satisfied with a more reasonable settlement than the commodore's less respectable women friends. And if this was so, William was quite right, for Frank took excellent care of her difficult spouse and was apparently content with her niggardly half million.

Yet if some saw William as shamelessly conniving and manipulative, it is nonetheless true that he did a great deal for his father. He was an effective steward of the railroads, and in the eight years that he survived the commodore he doubled the fortune. Some observers have argued that all he had to do was sit on it, like the dragon Fafnir in Wagner's *Ring* cycle, and let it grow, profiting more, in the crude phrase of the street, by his backside than his brain. Henry Clews, on the other hand, always maintained that the son was possessed of a fair share of the paternal genius and that holding that empire of lines together in an increasingly profitable union had taken almost as much skill as to assemble them. William's business techniques, however, were certainly different; he used patience, moderation, and reason where his father had used bluster and guile. It may have been a case of the perfect caretaker taking the place of the great pioneer. And William in the end may have been as good a son to the old man as he was undisputedly a good husband to his settled, dignified, God-fearing spouse and a good father to his eight handsome and devoted children.

But what about the will? Did he not "con" his father into leaving the great bulk of his estate away from his siblings? The will was written only two years before the commodore's death, when he was eighty-one and suffering from a variety of serious and painful ailments. Was there undue influence? The contestants never proved any, and the testator's reputation was certainly not that of an easily influenced man. He was known to have wanted his holdings kept together, and he had little affection for his other children, to whom, in any event, he bequeathed sums far greater, as Consuelo Balsan pointed out in her memoirs, than an English duke would have left his daughters or younger sons. It seems perfectly probable that William had been roundly told by his sire to take the will as drafted or leave it. He did settle with two contesting siblings for less than a million dollars, and he was supposed to have considerably sweetened the shares of the others, which, in view of the general acrimony and their bitter and baseless charges, seems more than most successful litigants would have done. And he personally carried the bonds representing the additional payments to each of his sisters. When one of his brothers-in-law facetiously pointed out that according to the late-afternoon prices he was $150 short of the amount promised, he quietly pulled out his pen and wrote a check for the balance. William always accepted people for what they were. He had not made the universe but he was going to live in it, and live in it as comfortably as he could.

In the last two decades of the commodore's life William had been firmly established as the heir-apparent, and this was reflected in his style of living, though it was nothing to what it would become after his father's death. We see him in a conversation piece by Seymour Guy, executed in 1873, in the living room of his Fifth Avenue house. The chamber is cluttered, comfortable, mid-Victorian. The elaborate candelabra over the fireplace, the romantic landscapes and anecdotal pictures on the yellow wall above the dark brown waist-high paneling, the big arched doorway disclosing another reception area shrouded in darkness, all suggest the solid ease and settled satisfaction of the arrived family. William, seated comfortably in a plush armchair, his back to the crackling fire, and his sober, placid wife, on the other side of the grate, an open book, perhaps a religious tract, in her lap, seem to have neither need nor desire for more sumptuous quarters or grander society, though both of these will be coming in time. No, they are quite content with their home and with the good-looking, well-dressed family of four sons, four daughters, and three in-laws, standing or sitting before them in poses for the artist.

These comely young people seem equally satisfied with their place in the world, but there is a difference. There is a distinct note of "This will do very well for *now*" in their attitude. One can see it in the regal figure of Margaret, the eldest daughter, dominating the center of the painting in a sweeping blue lace-trimmed gown beside her tall severe husband, Elliott Shepard, the strict sabbatarian who would not allow his streetcars to operate on Sunday. It is they who will build the vast dull palace in Scarborough (now the Sleepy Hollow Country Club) to house their dynasty. One can see it in the eldest son, Cornelius, leaning down to touch the wrist of his pretty wife, Alice. He does not yet suggest the pious churchman who will say his prayers at night in the largest mansions of New York and Newport, but it is evident that he has a will of his own. And Emily, a recent bride, allowing her white kid glove to be buttoned by Will Sloane, of the carpet family, will obviously be quite at home in the huge rambling structure of shingle that she will erect in Lenox, as will the self-confident little Lila in the even more extensive ones that her future husband will raise on thousands of wooded acres on Lake Champlain and in the Adirondacks. William K. and Florence, standing decoratively in the archway, seem ready to leave the old folks and "go on" to some party, no doubt given by swankier neighbors whose new châteaux on the avenue may presage "Marble House" in Newport and "Florham" in New Jersey. Frederick, standing behind his mother, still in his uncomfortable teens, seems a bit out of it, but only because he wants it that way. He will leave a greater fortune than any of his siblings, even though he will have only a younger son's portion. And little George, sharing the honors of the center of the scene with sister Margaret, might be dreaming of the fairy palace that he will build in the mountains of North Carolina, exhausting all of his heritage in one fell swoop. It will be the greatest of the Vanderbilt dwellings.

Surely no family, outside of royalties, will have been housed on such a scale. But I seem to make out a hint of sadness, or at least of skepticism, on the bland, matronly countenance of their mother, Maria Kissam Vanderbilt, who may have played the role of "Madame Mère," whose constant warning to the Bonaparte clan was *"Pourvu que cela dure."* One wonders if Maria would not have stopped the clock just where it was.

Where the children were headed is heralded in another conversation piece of the same decade, this one by Lucius Rossi, depicting the family of William Astor, then at the apex of the social pyramid. There is nothing in the least bourgeois about the ballroom in which the posed Astor ladies, reclining on Louis XV chairs, doll-like in Worth gowns, their tiny slippered feet resting on cushions, sip tea from obviously empty cups. The background here is almost awesomely aristocratic and European; we might be viewing the salon of a Roman palazzo or of an old *hôtel* in the Faubourg St. Germain. Between gilded Corinthian columns hangs the sixteenth-century portrait of some ruffed, royal personage. The only American note is struck by William Astor, bored with it all, holding his newspaper in hand as if to maintain some contact with a world despised by his womenfolk. William Henry Vanderbilt, still bourgeois, is still happy. The husband of *the* Mrs. Astor, engaged in a losing battle against conversion to the higher social state, is not. Only women could really enjoy the New York social life of the last half of the last century.

In 1873, when the Vanderbilt conversation piece was painted, the commodore was still very much alive. He was regarded with respect, fear, and even affection by William's sons, whom he very much liked, but only with respect and fear by the daughters. I doubt they were ashamed of him; they were all good women, strict in their deportment, honorable in their personal relations, and affectionate in their families. Neither they nor their brothers pined to be included in "high society"; that would be the province of their spouses. What they wanted was an ordered and respectable life, and the old ancestor, with his autocratic temper and foul tongue, was certainly in the way of that. It must have come as something of a relief, however unexpressed, when the commodore finally died in 1877, and the fortune was Papa's at last.

William, to assert the new rank of his family as the richest and presumably most powerful in the business community, directed the Herter brothers to build him a vast rococo brownstone on the corner of Fifty-first Street and Fifth Avenue, plus a twin, to be divided into two dwellings for his daughters, Margaret and Emily, directly to the north. William's house, known as No. 640, stripped many years later of its elaborate external trimmings and Frenchified by his granddaughter-in-law Grace, would become well known to later generations of New Yorkers. In his day, however, it was heavily pretentious, both inside and out, a great hodgepodge of styles, from Italian Renaissance to modern Japanese, chock-full of the works of some sixty sculptors and carvers, with columns four stories high of red African marble, front doors copied from Ghiberti, Roman balconies, and a mammoth malachite vase. William authorized, and presumably paid for, the splendid edition of a two-volume work, edited by Edward Strahan, entitled *Mr. Vanderbilt's House and Collection,* which began exuberantly as follows: "In these volumes we are permitted to make a revelation of a private home which better than any other possible selection may stand as a representative of the new impulse now felt in the national life. Like a more perfect Pompeii, the work will be the vision and image of a typical American residence, seized at the moment when the nation begins to have a taste of its own."

But even by the standards of our day, where the demand for "masterpieces" has restored to fashion every bygone school of art and rendered obsolete the old term "philistine," William's collection is a bad one. Storytelling academic canvases of the mid-nineteenth century, largely French, with such titles as "The Recruit," "The King's Favorite," "A Dream of Arabian Nights," "Attiring the Bride," and "Cupid's Whisper," by such forgotten masters as Zamaçois, Willems, Villegas, Leloir, and Lefebvre, filled the gallery in closely hung double rows. When the visitor happened upon an Alma-Tadema, a Boldini, a Bonheur, or a Gérôme, his heart must have taken a leap, and when he came to a Meissonier it must have seemed like a Titian!

William, as a collector, might have been the original of the man who "knows what he likes." Following in his father's footsteps, he bowed to no man in his judgment of depicted animals. "I don't know as much about the quality of the picture as I do about the action of those cattle," he told a French dealer about a rustic scene by Troyen. "I have seen them like that thousands of times."

Maria Vanderbilt was not impressed with the collection. She wrote to a friend: "I remember the first picture we ever bought. We paid ninety dollars for it, and we were afraid to let our friends know how extravagant we had been. I have the picture yet, and there is more pleasure to me in looking at it than all the Meissoniers and other great pictures in the house."

I wish we knew what that picture was. It may well have been the jewel of the collection. Meissonier, anyway, was her husband's favorite. He spent a total of $190,000 on the works of that military artist, including his own portrait, executed in the master's studio in Paris. The perfection of detail was particularly admired by the meticulous tycoon. What he saw in the great Napoleonic battle scenes was aptly described by Henry James in a piece on "Friedland":

It is hard, however, to admire it restrictively without seeming to admire it less than one really does. It seems to me it is a thing of parts rather than an interesting whole. The parts are admirable, and the more you analyse them the better they seem. The best thing, say, is a certain cuirassier, and in the cuirassier the best thing is his clothes, and in his clothes the best thing is his leather straps, and in his leather straps the best thing is the buckles. This is the kind of work you find yourself performing over the picture; you may go on indefinitely. That great general impression which, first and foremost, it is the duty of an excellent picture to give you, seems to me to be wanting here. M.

Meissonier is the great archaeologist of the Napoleonic era; he understands to a buttonhole the uniform of the Grand Army.

William, in any event, derived an immense pleasure from his paintings and loved to roam in his gallery and show them off to his children and grandchildren. One sees him and his wife greeting their friends and those of their offspring in the big, dark, glinting reception rooms in the middle of the afternoon, with all the thick curtains drawn, as was the custom of the day, perfectly content with their callers and quite indifferent to the more stylish society up and down the avenue outside, which envied and sneered but would soon enough engulf them.

William died in his Grecian library of apoplexy at the age of sixty-three. The remark for which he is most remembered, "The public be damned," has been notoriously misunderstood. What he meant was that his first and preemptive duty was to his stockholders. But his stockholders were largely himself and his family.

CORNELIUS II
AND
CHAUNCEY DEPEW

The Breakers, Newport, Rhode Island.

WILLIAM HENRY VANDERBILT in his will, disposing of some two hundred million dollars, the largest fortune in America if not in the world, followed to some extent his father's principle of primogeniture. The commodore had said to Chauncey Depew shortly before he died: "I would like if I could be assured that some Vanderbilt would be in the management of the New York Central for many generations to come, but I do not hope that the Vanderbilt influence will extend beyond the sons of my son, William H." William knew that his own estate, which was already more than twice the size of his father's, was too vast to be handled by a single legatee, so, like some of the later Roman emperors, he decided to divide the empire. A division between his four sons and four daughters, or even between his four sons, would have too much fragmented the fortune, so he split it between the two oldest, Cornelius II and William K., marking the former as titular head of the family by an extra legacy of two million. He did not, however, treat the rest of his progeny as meagerly as the commodore had his. The other six received ten million apiece, which allowed them, in that era of small imposts and high purchasing dollars, to live almost as grandly as their more favored siblings. Indeed, George's lifestyle was to be the grandest of all.

Cornelius II had been the perfect crown prince; he now became the perfect monarch. Handsome, serious, high-minded, industrious, efficient, and thorough, he had already long shown his abilities in the administrative offices of the New York Central. He had got on well with his grandfather—no easy task—and with his father—a much easier one—and his wife, Alice, seemed to conceive of no nobler role in life than that of consort of the chief of a great capitalistic clan. Both took with the utmost gravity what they regarded as the duties of their position as business and social leaders. If there was an aspect of humorlessness in their attitude—well, one couldn't expect them to have everything. And a sense of humor has never been a necessary attribute of power.

Whatever the austerities of their public image, in private they enjoyed a warm and close family relationship. Certainly their children adored them. It is true that Cornelius III, "Neily," broke bitterly with his father and that the breach was not healed before the latter's premature death, for reasons to be explored in a later chapter, but the very violence of the quarrel (over the woman Neily married) sprang from the closeness of the relationship that had preceded it and Neily's outrage that his parents should so oppose him when he most needed and expected their love. The other children, even while feeling that Neily was being treated a bit roughly, nonetheless implored him to consider what his imperviousness to the paternal will was doing to their father's health and state of mind. Cornelius's daughter, Gladys, would never let anyone so much as glimpse a Sargent portrait of her father which she had inherited, because she deemed it an unflattering resemblance. And the fact that Alice Vanderbilt shared few of the artistic or literary tastes of her sculptor daughter, Gertrude Whitney, had no effect on the latter's deep and constantly expressed devotion to her. It is not surprising that Neily never quite recovered from the quarrel that his father's early death kept him from making up.

With William Henry's death and the distribution of his estate, Cornelius and Alice took steps to establish their supremacy in the clan. William K., goaded by his wife, Alva, had stolen a lead by erecting the hitherto grandest of the Vanderbilt mansions, a gray French Renaissance château on Fifty-second Street and Fifth Avenue, and celebrating its completion with a famous costume ball. Cornelius had attended as Louis XVI and Alice as the "electric light," evocations of a romantic past and a shining future equally inappropriate for a couple so solidly representative of a very established present. But the time had now come for the older brother to set the pace.

Cornelius had already built a relatively modest dwelling on Fifty-seventh Street and Fifth Avenue. This he commissioned George Post to expand into the largest private residence in the city. Like Richard

Morris Hunt, Alva's architect, Post received his inspiration from the royal châteaux of the Loire Valley, particularly Blois, and his edifice of red brick with its fine square tower, its entrance court and grilled gates opening on Grand Army Plaza, soon covered the whole block front on the avenue between Fifty-seventh and Fifty-eighth streets. A European visitor, ignorant of the nature of our republic, might have assumed, standing by the victorious equestrian statue of General Sherman at the southeast end of Central Park and facing the Vanderbilt entrance, that he was viewing the palace of the sovereign of the city.

One is not surprised to learn that Alice Vanderbilt was indignant when the city fathers permitted the statue of the nude lady surmounting the fountain in the square to present her backside to her bedroom. But the Vanderbilts, unlike the Medicis in Florence to whom they were in some ways analogous, had little political power, and the lady did not change her posture. Indeed she survives to this day, presenting the same portion of her anatomy to the white façade of the Bergdorf-Goodman store, as if to demonstrate that a fine female figure has no need of fancy gowns.

Cornelius and Alice made lavish use of the talents of John La Farge and Saint-Gaudens to embellish their vast interior, but although the individual artifacts may have been well enough, their cumulative effect, to judge from photographs, was not happy. The rooms were heavy, cluttered, pontifical. The proprietors seemed more interested in impressing their visitors with grandeur than with beauty, a common fault in houses of the day. The same is true of The Breakers, the Genovese palazzo that Hunt created for them in Newport, largest of the villas in that summer community and visited today by thousands of tourists. "Why," some of them must ask, gaping up at the beetling stories of marble and contrasting the magnitude of the structure with the meanness of its park and garden, "did they want anything so huge?"

I can remember in 1938, at a debutante party given at The Breakers by Cornelius and Alice's daughter, Countess László Széchényi, talking to an old cotillion leader of the Mauve Decade who sniffed at the slender show of servants and recalled nostalgically the time when a footman in the maroon livery of the Vanderbilt family had been stationed on each step of the great marble stairway. He made me think of one of those romantic musical movies, popular at the time, in which

Jeanette MacDonald and Nelson Eddy were dressed up as royalties. But how could two such serious persons as Cornelius and Alice have been involved in such games of make-believe? And what did they imagine such a life would do to their children?

I can only suppose that they really believed that it was the duty of leaders of society to entertain according to the fashions of the day. It was not enough to go regularly to church, to give generously to the poor, to maintain the strictest moral standards and set an example in one's speech and decorum. No, one had to provide some bread and circuses, too, not necessarily for the mob, but for "society," a group presumably made up of the community's responsible leaders.

One of Alice's nieces described her to me as "pompous," but an old gentleman who had known her well insisted that, on the contrary, she had been a "dear little lady, very definite and straightforward, with no airs at all." Yet both descriptions might have been true, as they both might have been true of Queen Victoria. Alice's supposed pomposity might have consisted only in her concept of the role she deemed it her duty to fulfill. It is possible that she might not have even wanted the role, but accepted the fate that had assigned it to her. One must remember that a large number of her most respected contemporaries believed that she and her husband were performing a valuable service to the community in being just what they were. Most of us are capable of turning anything we want to do, or don't want to do, into an obligation. As A. C. Bradley wrote of Macbeth, he may have murdered Duncan, basically against his own will and better judgment, as a kind of appalling duty.

The man who more than any other created the public image of Cornelius II as a dedicated public servant was Chauncey Depew, attorney for and later president of the New York Central. He worked for the Vanderbilts during most of his long life, having turned down the ministry to Japan at the urgency of the commodore, whose lawyer and principal assistant he had then become, working with the old man, at his home or office, every day in the last ten years of his life, the decade in which three-quarters of the great fortune was made. Half a century later Depew was still on the job, a "grand old man" with large piercing eyes and an aquiline nose, a tall gleaming bald dome and thin, gravely smiling lips, the high priest of the railroad interests who had even got himself elected to the United States Senate to further their cause, the ultimate apologist of *laissez-faire,* the smooth promoter of great ends over small means, the genial idealist at banquets, the sharp realist in the smoke-filled rooms, hailed by all as the greatest after-dinner speaker of his time.

Depew could never sufficiently express his admiration for the family to whom he had dedicated his life. In his sonorous phrases one catches a whiff of the smoke from the altars of the era. But if the commodore was the greatest, ranked by Depew with Lincoln, Grant, Sherman, and Sheridan, it was his grandson, Cornelius II, whom the old lawyer most revered: "It was my good fortune and my happiness to be intimate with him from the time of his entrance into the railway service in his early life until his death. He was so modest and retiring, so shunned publicity that he was little understood. He was one of the most charitable, thoughtful, wisely philanthropic and courageous of men."

With the death of Cornelius II in 1899 at the age of only fifty-six, the Vanderbilt dynasty at the New York Central really came to an end. The family influence through stock ownership would be felt throughout the first four decades of this century, and William K., both senior and junior, Harold, and Alfred would play roles of varying importance, but the sense of a family leader was gone. No other member applied the mystique to the role that Cornelius had. His brother William K. was too much of a pleasant realist ever to dream that a locomotive could be anything more than a locomotive, or a fancy-dress ball anything more than a frolic.

Alice survived the husband to whom she referred, even to her grandchildren, as "Mr. Vanderbilt," for almost four decades, a widowhood equal to Queen Victoria's. She inhabited The Breakers until the end, but high taxes and tempting purchase offers induced her at last to sell the Fifty-eighth Street house and move ten blocks up the avenue to the smaller mansion of the late George Gould. She survived three of her sons—William, who had died when still at Yale; Reginald, an alcoholic; and Alfred, who was drowned on the *Lusitania*—and the breach with Neily, though patched up, always left scars. Her two daughters, however, and many grandchildren consoled her in old age.

I seem to catch a glimpse of her in Gloria Morgan Vanderbilt's dubiously entitled memoirs, *Without Prejudice*. She relates that at a dinner at The Breakers, when Alice learned that her beautiful young daughter-in-law (later to bring so much trouble to the family) had no pearls, she told the butler to bring her a pair of scissors, and undoing her own necklace she snipped off a long strand, which she then handed to Gloria with the grave announcement, "All the Vanderbilt women have pearls."

WILLIAM K.
AND
ALVA

The William Henry Vanderbilt family in Newport (c.1886).
Alva, with black scarf, seated on the step to the left and
behind W. Seward Webb; William K. standing far right;
Consuelo seated on the step to the right with George;
William Henry and Maria enthroned center.

THE EVOLUTION of brownstone society in late-nineteenth-century New York, as we have seen, was a rapid one. First came the robber barons, caring for little but their money-making, securing their goals at any cost, with usually subdued, obedient spouses. But the latter were soon succeeded by more glittering daughters-in-law or granddaughters who built vast and vaster palaces and helped to fabricate the elaborate net of etiquette in which the sons and grandsons of the original tycoons would be as hopelessly enmeshed as the French nobles by the Sun King's Versailles. For these poor souls, lacking the vigor or motivation of the founders, were inclined to take refuge, at best, in such occupations as horse breeding or yacht racing, or, at worst, in adultery, gambling, or drink, anything to escape the monstrous social preoccupations of their mates.

I know that my wife's grandfather used to be summoned from the Knickerbocker Club, where he repaired to play cards after leaving his office, by a call from his butler to remind him to be home in time to get dressed for dinner on nights when his wife was entertaining. It was the revenge, you might say, of the female for the earlier bondage of her sex while the money was being amassed.

William K. Vanderbilt, second son of William Henry and Maria, found himself in this predicament. With his older brother, Cornelius, he had divided the bulk of their father's fortune (the six other siblings receiving only ten million apiece), which, added to his good looks, charm, and easy affable manners, made him one of the most eligible bachelors of the planet. He was a good businessman, too, very helpful in the New York Central office, and, unlike his father, he even had an eye for art, if a conventional one, as his purchase of Rembrandt's

"Grand Turk" would indicate. I see him as suave, tolerant, with smiling eyes, kind, indulgent—too indulgent, perhaps, with his family—overwilling to make concessions to avoid scenes, tending to become really serious only with his horse trainer or yacht skipper, overanxious not to be bothered with pesky details or family squabbles, never fully engaged with life, mildly melancholy. He confessed once to a reporter: "My life was never destined to be quite happy. It was laid out along lines which I could not foresee almost from earliest childhood. It has left me with nothing to hope for, with nothing definite to seek or strive for. Inherited wealth is a real handicap to happiness. It is as certain death to ambition as cocaine is to morality."

Such a man was the natural prey of such a woman as Alva Smith. She was subject to no such melancholy reflections on the issue of inherited wealth. Her only concern was whether it was ample enough to buy all the dukes and build all the palaces her insatiable ego required.

There were no ambitions in that day fiercer than those of the old Southern gentry ruined by the war; the heroine of *Gone With the Wind* is their prototype. Alva, daughter of Murray Forbes Smith, an Alabama cotton planter who had tried to resuscitate his fallen fortunes in Paris, and of Phoebe Ann, a Kentucky Desha (Lyndon Baines Johnson was a scion of that clan), was possessed of all of Scarlett O'Hara's grim determination to climb back to the top of the social heap. And it took some climbing, too, for when Paris had proved unfruitful, the Smiths had been reduced to running a boardinghouse in New York. Alva, however, knew how to play even a bad hand, and she had a trump card in her friend, Consuelo Ysnaga, a Cuban heiress who had married Lord Mandeville, heir of the duke of Manchester. Armed with a few such connections, she was later to say, as if *she* had been the one to do the stooping, "I was the first of my set to marry a Vanderbilt." Gore Vidal, putting her into his witty novel *Empire* at a later stage of her career, has her add two other "firsts": divorcing her husband and marrying a Jew (Oliver Belmont).

How did she ever catch a man as attractive and sought after as William K.? One can see in the photograph of her at her great costume ball of 1883, when she was thirty, that she had some looks, but the temper and stubbornness are also apparent, and she was to lose the looks early. "I hear you're saying I look like a frog," she reproached her friend, Mamie Fish. "A toad, dear, a toad." And indeed the toad is what that square staring countenance suggests. I suspect it was the force of her character and the vigor of her conversation that intrigued first William K. and later Belmont. Alva had humor, too; she could laugh at herself as well as make mock of others. There is something fascinating to world-weary second-generation heirs in a woman with the energy of their forebears, who knows just what she wants and just how to get it.

What Alva lacked was imagination. She was incapable of foreseeing that bullying her daughter into a marriage she didn't want would bring her daughter no happiness and herself no satisfaction. Nor was she able to predict that, having pushed herself up to the top of the social ladder, she would find only ennui at that bleak altitude. Like Lady Macbeth, she was so intent on the means that she lost all vision of what the ends would amount to. But Alva was also very intelligent. When she saw what she had done to her daughter, she did her utmost to help her redo her life, and when she saw what she had done to herself, she tossed society to the winds and threw herself into the great cause of women's suffrage, where she made a name for herself that endures to our day.

But to return to the bride of William K.: having become Mrs. Vanderbilt, she was determined to build the finest house in New York and to give the greatest parties there. In both aims she succeeded. Richard Morris Hunt regarded the château that he designed for her on Fifth Avenue, inspired in part by Blois, but perhaps even more by the mansion of Jacques Coeur in Bourges, as his masterpiece. Critics then and since have insisted that such an edifice was more for kings than burghers and that it should have been surrounded by a vast park, but Alva and Hunt knew what they were doing. Jacques Coeur was a fourteenth-century Vanderbilt; he had put up his big house in the very center of his hometown.

It was in this château that Alva gave the costume party that supposedly marked the social arrival of the Vanderbilts. Accounts of it are always accompanied by the telling of the legend of how she maneuvered Mrs. William B. Astor (known simply as "Mrs. Astor") into calling on her by allowing the latter's young daughter, Caroline, to rehearse for a quadrille until her heart was quite set on it and then letting it be known, with feigned regret, that it was a pity that the girl should have wasted her time as she (Alva) could hardly be expected to invite to her party the daughter of a lady who had never so much as acknowledged her existence. What the legend does not tell is that Mrs. Astor would have called on Alva soon enough, trick or no trick. Nobody was going to keep a young couple as rich and attractive and hospitable as the Vanderbilts out of society indefinitely. One could have found, no doubt, impregnable little enclaves of frozen titled society in Paris, Vienna, or Rome, but the Four Hundred, like the human body, was made up of constantly changing units. The fact that I can find no better term for it than a number that does not even measure its quantity shows what an amorphous entity it was. Not everybody, of course, even among the very rich, could get into New York society. It was perfectly possible for a multimillionaire to be too boorish or too crooked or too eccentric or too loose to be tolerated. But almost any family of goodwill, good manners, and large bank account could expect to be admitted after a certain waiting period. How else could society have survived?

The crudeness and force with which Alva, in 1895, went after the ninth duke of Marlborough as a husband for her daughter, Consuelo (named, of course, for Lady Mandeville), is without example in the mild annals of New York and Newport social life. She not only vilified the character of Winthrop Rutherfurd, the unexceptionable gentleman with whom her seventeen-year-old child was understandably and appropriately in love; she virtually imprisoned Consuelo in a home where no dissenting opinion was allowed to penetrate. Consuelo later wrote that her mother's rages were so frightening "that she might indeed easily suffer a stroke or a heart attack if further provoked."

Why did such tactics succeed? The duke himself was hardly an aggressive suitor. He made no secret of his financial needs, having the biggest house in England to keep up, or of the fact that he, too, had to sacrifice a deeper affection. He wasn't even attracted to Consuelo's remarkable beauty. "I don't like tall women," he retorted, years later, to someone who was admiring his wife's looks. He must have hated (if he ever saw it) Max Beerbohm's cartoon of the bridal couple, showing him as a near dwarf beside his splendid spouse. When Sargent painted the Marlboroughs at Blenheim, he posed them on the stairway of the great hall so that the duchess's superior height might seem attributable to her standing on a higher step. It would not have taken much of a rebuff on Consuelo's part to induce this languid peer to transfer his addresses to a more willing heiress.

But the rebuff did not come, even though Consuelo knew just what the duke was after, even when her twelve-year-old brother Harold told her with a boy's frankness, "He's only marrying you for your money." It seems remarkable, particularly in view of the strong character that she later showed. But one must remember her tender age and the brutality of a mother who could still manage to make herself loved and respected as well as feared. Consuelo always remained fond of the parent of whom she could nonetheless write:

In my youth, children were to be seen but not heard; implicit obedience was an obligation from which one could not conscientiously escape. Indeed we suffered a severe and rigorous upbringing. Corporal punishment for minor delinquencies was frequently administered with a riding whip. I have a vivid memory of the last such lashing my legs received as I stood by while my mother wielded her crop. Being the elder, I had the privilege of the first taste of the whip—Willie followed. . . . I bore these punishments stoically, but such repressive measures bred inhibitions and even now I can trace their effects.

Consuelo's real tragedy was that her parents had just separated— the natural consequence of extreme incompatibility—and that Alva, keeping the children, had forbidden her estranged husband the house. Still, William K., who was supposed to have been angered by the idea that any pressure should be placed on his beloved daughter's freedom of choice, retained the whip hand. All he had to do was to close his checkbook, and the duke, perhaps even gratefully, would have taken his leave. But he didn't. Instead he agreed to settle millions on the young couple. Presumably he had been somehow convinced that Consuelo's "I will" would come from the heart. But it is hard not to suspect that his distaste for scenes was a factor in his crumbling before the demands of the termagant he had married.

Alva demonstrated the same force of character in obtaining her own "freedom" as she had in depriving Consuelo of hers. She was resolved not only to divorce William K. for adultery (of which we can at least hope the poor man had had the satisfaction), but to marry Oliver Belmont, himself a divorcé, and maintain intact her position in society. One begins to suspect that the setting up of hurdles in order to jump them was her way of adding a bit of zest to the sameness of a social game that was already showing itself a drag to her lively spirit. And were not the Belmonts partly Jewish? Better and better!

She called now on each of her husband's siblings to find out how they stood about the divorce. "I expect you to be on *my* side," she announced firmly to Emily Sloane. "I never take sides," was the latter's somewhat evasive reply. As none of them were willing to oppose the popular brother, Alva turned her back on the whole clan and refused to invite any Vanderbilt but her former mother-in-law to Consuelo's enormous wedding to the duke.

France was the Nevada of that day, and William K., like the gentleman he always too much was, allowed himself to be sued in an uncontested suit for adultery. It was arranged that he should be "surprised" with a demimondaine hired for the purpose, one Nellie Neustretter of Eureka, Nevada, then established in Paris. Henry James, hearing of the situation, jotted it down in the notebook where he kept his ideas for future fiction. The germ of a possible story (never actually written) that he drew from it seems in keeping with William K.'s charm:

. . . and the thing suggested by what was told me the other day of the circumstances of the W. K. Vanderbilt divorce: his engaging the demi-mondaine, in Paris, to *s'afficher* with him in order to force his virago of a wife to divorce him. I seem to see all sorts of things in that—a comedy, a little drama, of a fine colour, either theatrised or narrated; a subject, in short, if one turns it in a certain way. The way is, of course, that the husband doesn't care a straw for the *cocotte* and makes a bargain with her that is wholly independent of real intimacy. . . . The *femme galante* may take, of course, a tremendous, disinterested fancy to him.

Needless to say, after the divorce, Alva got her way. She married Belmont, and everyone came to their parties. They even had two Hunt mansions in Newport, for Marble House had been part of her divorce settlement, and he owned Belcourt, the curious villa-barn whose living quarters were situated over the stables of his peerless collection of carriage horses. Alva's life was proof of the simple proposition that you can get away with anything if you're bold enough to carry it off.

Someone who didn't get away with it was Alva's sister-in-law, Jessie Sloane, who had left her spouse, Henry (a brother of Emily Vanderbilt's husband, William), to marry Oliver Belmont's brother, Perry. But her vision was clouded by passion, something that, at least in the sexual sense, presented little problem to Alva. Jessie abandoned not only her husband but two small daughters, and society slammed its doors to her. Years later, when Alva's daughter Emily married a French baron, Amaury de la Grange, he asked to be presented to her mother. When told that Mrs. Belmont was not accepted by the family, he still insisted. In France, he pointed out, society may reject an erring member; the family, never.

Oliver Belmont died, prematurely, in 1908, and Alva's real life began. For she found a field at last in which her hot temper and aggressiveness were sparkling virtues: the war for women's rights. From the very start of the suffragette movement in England and in the United States, she took the extreme belligerent position, scorning all compromise. "Mrs. Pankhurst is the greatest woman of the age," she snapped at reporters who met her on the dock in Southampton. "You will probably kill her, just as Joan of Arc was killed!"

Even when the Nineteenth Amendment had been passed, Alva cautioned women not to exercise their franchise until the political parties had been wrested from the monopoly of the male sex. "Beware of political pitfalls," she exhorted them. "Don't let either of the two old parties use you as cat's paws. Ignore their flattery. . . . Hand back to the wily leaders the empty honors offered. . . . You will be free to act at the right moment! Don't vote!"

Alva died in 1933 at the age of eighty, and the militant women who escorted her casket to its burial site carried banners with the motto "Failure is impossible."

William K. had died thirteen years earlier. A character in one of Oscar Wilde's comedies quips that good Americans go to Paris when they die. Neither William K. nor his former spouse had waited. Both were French residents at the end.

Consuelo described her father's death:

I was with him to the end. Whatever his sufferings he made no complaints; not even a gesture of ill-humor troubled the serenity he seemed to emanate. There was a fineness about him that one sensed clearly, and it seemed to me that nothing ignoble would ever touch him. In his business and in his life he lived up to the high standard of integrity he had set himself. I remember the tribute the duc de Gramont, one of France's leading sportsmen, paid him when he came to present his condolences: "I wish to express the grief of the French Jockey Club at your father's death. It is fine and honorable sportsmen such as he, mindful of the best traditions of the turf, we delight in welcoming. His death will be a great loss to the French racing world."

French sportsmen, then, and women the world over, owed some debt to a couple who found themselves in separation.

GEORGE
AND
RICHARD MORRIS HUNT

George W. Vanderbilt by James McNeill Whistler.

THEY ARE forever bracketed by Biltmore, one of the finest of the architect's creations and the grandest of the Vanderbilt houses. For each, this fairy castle, high in the mountains of western North Carolina, dominating more than a hundred thousand acres of forests and landscaped countryside, plus a whole community of farms, greenhouses, and supporting buildings, was to provide a life's climax—and, to some extent, an anticlimax.

In 1890, when building started on the project, the architect was sixty-three and his client twenty-eight. The latter had already traveled with the Hunts in Europe to be advised in the purchases needed to furnish so vast an edifice. Hunt had even taken him to Chantilly to meet the duc d'Aumale, son of Louis-Philippe, who had recently donated to the Institut de France his renovated palace with its whole splendid collection. The young George, looking around, must have had ideas of what he, too, could do on this scale. His mentor became more than a friend, almost a father figure.

Richard Morris Hunt had much the same sort of international upbringing as William and Henry James and the painter John Singer Sargent. The son of a Vermont congressman who had died young, he had been taken with his siblings by a restless, vigorous widowed mother to Europe, where the family means would go further and the cultural opportunities were greater. It was an itinerant life of constantly changing schools, pensions, and rented villas, of learning languages, of indefatigable sight-seeing, of varied and stimulating societies. It has always seemed to me a delightful way to grow up, but I suppose not all young people would agree, and certainly two of Richard's brothers (one, the painter William Morris Hunt) committed suicide in middle life. Richard himself, at any rate, seems to have made the most of his European opportunities, and when he did return to his native land, a graduate of the École des Beaux-Arts, to set up his office in New York, just prior to the Civil War, he dazzled the girls and threw envy into the hearts of less elegant youths with his dashing mustache and goatee, his military posture, his perfect French accent, his wit, and his abounding self-confidence.

He had some of the same ebullience and pungent conversational manner later to be shown by the young Theodore Roosevelt. He drew wide attention in social circles and became famous on the basis of a surprisingly small number of early commissions. The guardians of the pretty young heiress to a shipping fortune, Catherine Howland, it is true, were at first averse to the attentions shown her by this "arty" and "foreign" suitor, but, like everyone else, they came around, and the match was a lifelong and happy one. Hunt had come to beautify America, and America had better submit.

There was, however, one major check. During the war, for the fighting of which, like so many busy men, he purchased a substitute, he designed four grandiloquent Beaux-Arts gateways to the new Central Park which were rejected by the commissioners as insufficiently "American." The published designs had aroused considerable feeling among those who thought that "our lovely, rural, *natural* park" would be ruined forever by the intrusion of these pompous monuments of a monarchical Europe. And perhaps they had a point. If Hunt was, as his biographer Paul Baker put it, an ambassador from the Old World to the New, the New World had to be concerned that its spirit should not be overshadowed or oppressed.

The opposition of the commissioners, however, seems not to have been expressed by other clients, public or private. The era of expansion in all fields that followed the war was favorable to Hunt's ideas of grandeur. The new tycoons, in particular, allowed him to develop his ideas and were happy to provide unlimited sums for the purpose.

In this respect it is not necessary to take too literally what the architect's son and associate, Richard Howland Hunt, used to quote his father as saying: "It's your clients' money you're spending. Your business is to get the best result you can following their wishes. If they want you to build a house upside down, standing on its chimney, it is up to you to do it and still get the best possible result." For who would have dared ask anything like that of the great artist shown in the Sargent portrait standing in the hall of Biltmore, a cape thrown in lordly fashion over one shoulder, a clenched fist resting on the marble balustrade, those fine deep eyes piercing the beholder! And imagine the contemptuous stare one would have received from the master who, even in his youth, had been allowed by the French authorities to design the façade of one of the pavilions of the renovated Louvre. On the contrary, I imagine that the Yankee burgher, more interested in conspicuous consumption than in the development of indigenous architecture, would have come to Hunt only to order a Hunt palace. "So long as it's medieval!" was the single condition one client was reputed to have specified. What was good enough for Mrs. Astor was good enough for all.

Something else that contributed to the respect accorded to Hunt by the new rich was the business aspect of his profession. No such one existed for the poet's, the painter's, the sculptor's. But the architect had to supervise the construction of his building, enter into the details of the contract, and sometimes even choose the site. He was a prime factor in the development of real estate worth millions, even when it was only a "cottage" in Newport. Hunt became an integral part of the great world of capital that dominated all American life. It was only fitting that the imposing monument erected in his memory should have been placed on the avenue in Manhattan that had become the symbol of financial and social power.

It was inevitable that Hunt should become the architect of the Vanderbilts; never had nature ordained a more fitting symbiosis. William K. Vanderbilt's gray château on Fifth Avenue, and his Marble House and Cornelius II's Genovese palazzo in Newport set new standards in European splendor. The Vanderbilts slept in death in a Hunt mausoleum on Staten Island; even in divorce they could not escape him, as Alva found when she moved into her second husband's house, Belcourt. When you look at the photograph of Hunt at Alva's great costume ball, garbed ironically as Cimabue, the painter whom Dante chose to symbolize the transience of fame, it is tempting to fancy that the artist in the man was laughing at the fancy-dress world he had helped to create, with all its railroad magnates and their buxom mates beruffed and befeathered as monarchs, and wondering if it would not be carried off in a clap of time, leaving not a wrack behind.

He must anyway have had *some* doubts. There were plenty of critics of his day who carped at his derivative mansions. Even if they were handsome, did they have a real function other than being conspicuous? Henry James, revisiting his native land in 1905 after twenty years abroad, was struck by the seeming pointlessness of New York's display of wealth. "The scene of our feast was a palace, and the perfection of setting and service absolute. . . . The material pitch was so high that it carried with it no social sequence, no application, and that, as a tribute to the ideal, to the exquisite, it wanted company, support, some sort of consecration." The only thing, he suggested, that would have justified such a banquet was a "great court function" to "go on to."

The novelist felt much the same way about Newport, whose new villas he likened to "white elephants." "They look queer and conscious and lumpish—some of them, as with an air of the brandished proboscis, really grotesque—while their averted owners, roused from a witless dream, wonder what in the world is to be done with them. The answer to which, I think, can only be that there is absolutely nothing to be done; nothing but to let them stand there always, vast and blank, for reminder to those concerned of the prohibited degrees of witlessness, and the peculiarly awkward vengeances of affronted proportion and discretion." And stand indeed they do to this day, maintained by the Newport Preservation Society and displayed to countless busloads of admiring tourists who probably view them more with Hunt's eye than James's.

There was, however, one criticism of his country houses, at least in Newport, to which Hunt could not take exception: that they lacked the accessories and surroundings of their European counterparts. This, I am sure, he could only regret. No one knew better than he what Chenonceaux owed to a river or Chambord to a park of twenty miles' girth, and he must have yearned, particularly in his later years, for a patron who would at last give him the chance to show what he could do with limitless wealth and land at his disposal. And this was precisely what he saw in the dream of George Vanderbilt.

The youngest of William Henry's eight children was a gentle youth, more serious and studious than his older siblings and something of a mother's boy. The diary of his thirteenth year contains constant resolutions to read his Bible and to make more effort to deserve the love of his family and friends. Here are some typical entries for the year 1875:

I read my Bible this morning and began Isaiah and I think that was what made me feel so happy through the day.

I have been reading a book this afternoon from which I ought to learn a very useful lesson of truth and gaining control over my temper, but I can do nothing without God's help because if I rely on my own resolution I am sure to fail.

I don't think I have spent today as I should have done. I have trusted too much in my own ability and not enough in Jesus.

The Sun said that there were two thousand people at the house [for his brother Willy's wedding] and that the presents were worth half a million of dollars, neither of which were true.

I bought a floater, line, and hook this morning all for thirty cents; Mother gave me a dollar as she had no smaller change and when I took the seventy cents back to her she said I could keep it.

With the diary is a cashbook in which George carefully recorded every receipt and expenditure, even including a penny for a stamp. If he was later to become the most extravagant of the Vanderbilts, it was not from any lack of early training. He grew up to be something of a scholar, deeply interested in languages (he spoke six) and in esoteric literature, and prone to cultivate the society of artists and writers. Whistler painted him with a thin, elegant figure and brooding dark eyes, holding a riding crop between tapering fingers, the portrait of a dilettante. Sargent depicted him, more kindly, as a pale bookworm, the same long fingers inserted between the leaves of a folio. George liked to translate modern prose into ancient Greek. But he was also a big-game hunter and was later to prove himself something of an expert in Indian dialects, forestry, and farming. Primarily, however, he had the soul of an artist, an artist without an art. Is that a dilettante? Not necessarily. There is nothing of the dilettante about Biltmore. It is simply too big.

Furthermore it cost him his fortune. George received only what his sisters did under William Henry's will: five million outright and five in trust. At his death in 1914, aged only fifty-two, the untouchable trust passed to his daughter, Cornelia, but his estate consisted of Biltmore. It is true that under the capable administration of his two Cecil grandsons Biltmore has today become a thriving and self-sufficient center for important forestry and farming development as well as tourism, but in the early 1900s it was widely known as "Vanderbilt's Folly." What, people asked, had possessed the poorest of the Vanderbilts to erect the biggest of their abodes?

He must have dreamed as a youth of doing something that would distinguish him from the rest of the family. Like his parents he had little interest in society. When his father died, he lived for a time with his mother, whom he adored, preferring for their summers the beauties of the Maine coast to the glister of Newport. He had little interest in business; he preferred traveling to exotic spots. When he met Hunt, who was working on so many of his family's projects, and came under the spell of that vigorous and eclectic imagination, he conceived his vision of what he and the great architect might do in the high French Renaissance style, freed of the restrictions of Fifth and Bellevue avenues. It was a great gamble, of course, for a young man to take, but who is to say it was not worth it? Biltmore has brought George a kind of immortality.

He may have closed his eyes and murmured a Nunc Dimittis when in 1907 he read this description of his home in Henry James's *The American Scene*:

I had, by a deviation, spent a week in a castle of enchantment; but if this modern miracle, of which the mountains of North Carolina happened to be the scene, would have been almost anywhere miraculous, I could at least take it as testifying, all relevantly, all directly, for the presence, as distinguished from the absence, of feature. One felt how, in this light, the extent and the splendor of such a place was but a detail; these things were accidents without which the great effect, the element that, in the beautiful empty air, made all the difference, would still have prevailed. What was this element but just the affirmation of resources?—made with great emphasis indeed, but in a clear and exemplary way; so that if large wealth represented some of them, an idea, a fine cluster of ideas, a will, a purpose, a patience, an intelligence, a store of knowledge, immediately workable things, represented the others.

It is just as well that George never saw what James wrote in a letter just after his visit: "Roll three or four Rothschild houses into one, surround them with a principality of mountain, lake and forest, 200,000 acres, surround *that* with vast states of niggery desolation and make it impossible, through distance and time, to get anyone to stay with you, and you have the bloated Biltmore . . . utterly unaddressed to any possible arrangement of life or state of society."

In fairness to both James and George it should be pointed out that James, during his visit, suffered from an agonizing gout attack and a snowstorm of unprecedented violence, and that the description of Biltmore in his book, written later, may have been "emotion recollected in tranquillity."

The portrait, already referred to, which George commissioned Sargent to paint of his architect to hang in Biltmore shows Hunt already in declining health. As Catherine Hunt, in her still unpublished life of her husband, wrote, the painter seemed "to have divined, apparently without knowing it himself, how much more ill Richard was than we realized. . . . The portrait represents a man thin and worn from suffering, and, though it has a certain likeness, the fire, the vigor and the personality are all wanting." After Hunt's death, not long afterwards in 1895, the artist offered to do a replica of the head for the widow, but she could not bear to have it.

Indeed it seems that Hunt's devotion to the Vanderbilts may have actually hastened his end. As Catherine wrote:

Mrs. William H. Vanderbilt had made a great point of our going to Lenox to the wedding of her granddaughter Adele Sloane to James Burden. The extremely hot days spent in Washington had been very exhausting [Ed.: where Hunt had gone to help George consider the Foulke tapestries for Biltmore], and the Lenox excursion seemed unwise, but Richard was determined to go and enjoyed every moment of the occasion. We left Elm Court [the Sloane estate] in a drizzling rain and Richard, always impatient when it was a question of catching a train, would not wait for the carriage next in line, but got on the box of the carriage which Esther and I were in, with the result that he must have gone back to New York in damp clothes. The next day we had a prolonged journey to Newport, with the result of an attack of gout, which continued to the end and kept him on the sofa in the morning room, from which he still transacted business.

Esther Hunt stayed with her father, but could not prevent his making a long professional visit to The Breakers and having a conference with that "exacting" lady, Mrs. Cornelius Vanderbilt II, who was "insistent" in her demands. This was followed by a rapid deterioration, and the end came in July.

Hunt did not live to see Biltmore acquire a chatelaine. This happened three years after his death when George, aged thirty-six, married Edith Stuyvesant Dresser. The couple had one child, Cornelia, who married an English nobleman, John Francis Amherst Cecil. George's widow inherited Biltmore, disposed of all but 12,500 acres of the estate, and opened it to tourists. It is now managed by Cornelia's two sons and, among historic American houses available to the public, it is second in popularity only to San Simeon, William Randolph Hearst's California mansion.

But however much I admire certain aspects of the houses of Hunt, there remains with me always a lingering impression of heaviness, of pomposity, almost at times of downright vulgarity. Even Biltmore, the finest of the lot, even when it dazzles, lies a bit weightily on the soul.

George's brother, William K., bequeathed to the Metropolitan Museum of Art Rembrandt's "Grand Turk," and it recently struck me that this painting has something in common with Biltmore. Of course, it is not the portrait of a Turk at all, grand or otherwise. It is the likeness of an old male model, swathed in the robes that the artist kept in his studio for just such a purpose, with a marvelous turban wrapped and rewrapped around his haughtily held head. The effect is no doubt splendid; the details are as meticulously wrought as the master could do. Yet there is something faintly ridiculous about it. We see that it's just an old Dutchman dressed up, and some of us might feel that he's too old and too sober-faced to be playing such a silly game. And so Biltmore, for all its glory, strikes me at times as engaged in charades in the North Carolina mountains. I have half a mind to tell it to go back to the Loire Valley. But would it really belong any better there?

THE DAUGHTERS
OF
WILLIAM HENRY

"House & Garden" at Elm Court, Lenox, Massachusetts—
the residence of Emily Vanderbilt (Sloane) White.

THERE WERE four of them—Margaret, Emily, Florence, and Eliza (Lila)—and they all lived to be old, their ages at the end ranging from seventy-six (Eliza) to ninety-eight (Florence). All married, more or less happily, and all survived their husbands (Emily survived two). All led quiet, regular, and rather stately lives in ostentatious mansions. Society columnists delighted in describing them (particularly Florence) as reserved, imposing, exclusive, strict, even "formidable" symbols of a more ordered and disciplined society which perhaps had never existed. In fact they were nice little old ladies, affectionate wives and mothers, who loved to play cards and give family house parties and who were not (except for Lila) in the least intellectual.

Margaret was the eldest, the one we see standing erect and rather queenlike in the center of the Seymour Guy conversation piece and whom Sargent painted later in imperial red. She had a much gentler and more accommodating nature than these poses would seem to imply. As a girl she had been embarrassed when the postman had delivered to her a letter addressed simply to "the richest girl in the world." She married Elliott Shepard, an exacting lawyer and rigid Presbyterian who owned a transit company which he allowed to suffer from the competition of others that permitted their cars to operate on Sunday. He was determined to build a mansion worthy of the dynasty he wished to establish, and he erected the grim monumental structure in Scarborough, New York, which is now the Sleepy Hollow Country Club. His extravagance cost his wife most of that part of her fortune that was not tied down in trust.

William Henry on his death in 1885 had left each of his daughters ten million dollars, half outright and half in trust. The half in trust had to be invested in bonds, with the result that the principal in each case amounted to the same sum on a daughter's death that it had on her father's, even though the life of the trust had encompassed the greatest rise in security values known to economic history. Margaret was obliged to sell her half of the northern twin of William Henry's brownstone to her sister Emily and move to an apartment thirty blocks north.

One of Elliott Shepard's grandsons told me: "I don't know if there's a hell, but if there is, Grandpa Shepard is surely in it." The stringency of this remark was caused by Shepard's having told one of his daughters that her physical deformity had been inflicted by God; whether as a test or punishment or even as an arcane blessing, it was not clear. But so severe were the injunctions of his Calvinist Deity that even after his demise his usually kind and tolerant widow was unable to bring herself to accept as the husband of her daughter Alice a member of the family that had run the Louisiana lottery, and the young couple had to elope. Eventually, however, Margaret came around and lived as cozily with Alice and her irreproachable husband as with the rest of her family. Indeed her daughter Louise had been made aware of a possible revision of her mother's attitude toward the exacting decedent when, after evoking a pious memory of her progenitor, she received only the chilling response, "Louise, your father has been dead for twenty-seven years."

Emily made a better match to handsome William Douglas Sloane, of the rug and furniture family. Mrs. Astor might have once said of the Sloanes, "Just because we walk on their carpets doesn't mean we must dine at their tables," but the utter respectability of this large and attractive clan soon gained it acceptance everywhere. Emily consolidated the two halves of the northern Vanderbilt twin into one vast house and built an even vaster shingle edifice in Lenox, Massachusetts, where she raised her three daughters and son. She was known for her agreeable disposition and her charities (she and her husband founded the Sloane Babies' Hospital) and her love of bridge. Seven years after Sloane's death in 1913 she married Henry White, the diplomat, though she was always afraid that she would not measure up to the standards of his brilliant and beautiful first wife. Indeed it is hard to imagine Emily, like her predecessor, as a member of the select and intellectual company known as the "Souls" in Edwardian society. But she and Harry, an affable and easygoing gentleman, were very happy together. He died in 1927, and she lived on for another score of years, faithful to her daily bridge game until her memory began to fade and she sat tranquilly reviewing pleasant, distant memories in an armchair by a table on which a single volume, Allan Nevins's life of White, reposed.

But she had one other diversion, which grew out of the passion in her family's blood for speed, as manifested in the commodore's fast vessels and locomotives and in the multitudinous race horses, racing cars, and sailing yachts of his descendants. In her nineties Emily liked to be driven as fast as her chauffeur dared down Lenox roads in the backseat of her high-roofed maroon Rolls-Royce town car.

Florence was the plainest, the dourest, the longest-lived, and by far the richest of the four. Her husband, Hamilton Twombly, like the man with the five talents in the parable, invested her money and his own so profitably in mining ventures that their joint fortunes rivaled those of Cornelius II and William K. Incidentally, Frederick, third son and only issueless child of William Henry, did the same with the five million he had inherited outright and died the richest of the Vanderbilts.

Florence looks handsome enough in Sargent's portrait, but one can tell by contemporary photographs that the artist flattered her. She built a huge Georgian house in New Jersey with an immense "pleasure dome" (her own term for it) containing a pool and indoor court for her daughter Ruth, and she owned as well the big stone and shingle villa on the Cliff Walk in Newport known as "Vinland." Moving from house to house at the same points in each year, with scores of servants and endless luggage, must have been in itself a life's occupation for the Vanderbilt sisters.

Legends grew up about Florence Twombly, tirelessly repeated by society columnists. John Mason Brown told me himself the story of his being sent home on Sunday night of a Labor Day weekend because his hostess declined to recognize the holiday. But perhaps she hadn't even known it existed. And in Newport it used to be said that the limousines lined up in her driveway well before 8:00 P.M. so that no dinner guest would affront his exacting hostess by being so much as a minute late. But summer colonies have a way of creating their own legends about the eccentricities of the wealthy and venerable; it adds a bit of color and spice to the banalities of the watering hole. And having invented them, they not only believe them; they act them out. I shouldn't be surprised to learn that Mrs. Twombly, looking out the window at the lineup on her drive, had asked what caused the traffic jam. Unless, of course, she herself had come to believe in the legend. Newport could be a masque.

The second Twombly daughter, Florence, married William A. M. Burden, a grandson of Henry Burden, the ironmaster of Troy. His first cousin, James A. Burden, had already married another grand-daughter of William Henry Vanderbilt, Florence Adele Sloane. The story of the Burden fortune, and how it was lost and recaptured by multiple marriages, reads like a Balzac novel. Henry Burden in the middle of the last century amassed a great capital from the manufacture of horseshoes. Cavalry needs in the Civil War gave his business an added boost, and it did not hurt that the commanding general of the Army of the Potomac, Irvin McDowell, had married his daughter Mary. But after his death his sons wasted much of their inheritance in a bitter family litigation. A common joke in New York was that the Burden fortune had passed to the lawyers, including Joseph H. Choate, who had written optimistically to his wife from Troy that Henry Burden himself had had a reputation for protracted lawsuits and that there was no reason to suppose that the suit between his sons would ever end.

The advent of the automobile completed the ruin that the family feud had started, and the third generation was saved only by the double Vanderbilt alliance. The fortune of the James Burdens suffered the usual attrition from estate duties, but the William Burden branch, thanks to the wise investments of Hamilton Twombly and his grandson, William A. M. Burden, Jr., remains wealthy to this day. The family saga would have pleased Balzac by even providing a crime. A great-grandson of Henry Burden was sentenced to jail in the 1930s for embezzlement.

Eliza, or "Lila" Vanderbilt, youngest of William Henry's daughters, was also the most cultivated, the prettiest, and the most amiable. Her marriage to Doctor Seward Webb was the Vanderbilts' first entry into what was considered an old Knickerbocker family. Seward's grandfa-ther had been an aide-de-camp of Washington. His father, a renowned journalist, was active in political circles; he was also something of a fire-eater and had engaged in several duels. Seward inherited some of his imperious nature. Armed with the fortune of a submissive and loving wife, he abandoned medicine and created a great domain in Shelburne, Vermont, on the shore of Lake Champlain. On many thousands of landscaped acres he established a cattle and horse farm with vast shingle barns, in one of which it was said a polo match could be played, and a long rambling house of gray stone and red shingle which looked out over a terraced garden to the lake and across to the Adirondacks where Webb had a camp with an even greater tract of land. But Shelburne Farms had none of the pomposity of other Vanderbilt residences. It was built to work, not to impress, and it fits into the countryside to this day, not modestly surely, but with the air of an assured and serene landed aristocrat. Webb was something of an artist.

He was also, unfortunately, something of a drug addict, which may have had a relation to the extremeness of his designs and ambitions. He made a large hole in his wife's fortune, but the land, waxing in value, passed to his descendants. His children, as the worldly phrase went, "married to advantage." Watson Webb became the husband of Electra Havemeyer, who created the Shelburne Museum, a treasury of Americana and also of some of the masterpieces of her mother's great collection of European painting. The summer guides speak in reverent tones of the Webbs, as of a kind of American royal family, giving to their commonest possessions the dignity of the Havemeyer artifacts. "This is a painting of Venice by Manet" is uttered in the same tone as "This is a portrait of Eliza Vanderbilt Webb by Munzio." Somehow, in Shelburne, one accepts it.

Lila Webb lived on in the big house at Shelburne Farms until 1936. She was known to the countryside as "Madame Webb," an ancient New England compliment rarely conferred on one not native-born.

HENRY WHITE

Elm Court.

H E DID NOT MARRY a Vanderbilt until 1920 when, a widower of seventy, he became the second husband of Emily Vanderbilt Sloane. But he seems to belong to the era I have so dubbed as its supreme diplomat, "the most useful man in the entire diplomatic service," in the words of Theodore Roosevelt. Henry ("Harry") White established the model of the State Department diplomat, in top hat and striped pants, who does his most effective business at weekends in historic country houses or in the corners of drawing rooms or even on the hunting field, who knows how to catch the right ear at just the right moment, and whose extensive acquaintance among the socially and politically great assures him of a private audience with any monarch, prime minister, or pope. There are two important lessons to be learned from Harry White's remarkable career: one, that it seems to have fitted almost no American legate but himself, and, two, that it has been blindly followed by generations of diplomats who have confused dinner parties and weekends with power.

He was born in 1850 of two old, honorable, and rich Maryland families. After his father's death when he was only three he lived with his mother and younger brother in Hampton, the home of his maternal grandparents, General and Mrs. Ridgely. This spacious mansion with a cupola rose above terraced lawns; its sixty-foot-long hall was hung with family portraits, including a Sully of Mrs. Ridgely as a young girl playing a harp. His grandmother would take him with her, dressed in white ducks, when she went calling in the neighborhood in her landau drawn by four smart horses with a footman—a slave, of course— clinging behind. The slaves at Hampton were supposed to have been kindly treated, but young Harry remembered his grandfather boxing the ears of a groom for a trivial offense and the forced cutting off of the hair of a mulatto girl, who was almost white, because it was not "woolly" enough. The family, needless to say, was thoroughly Southern in its sympathies: if Harry was taken at six to call on President Pierce it was because the chief executive was deemed a "sound" Northerner, and if the Ridgelys spent their summers in Newport it was because that resort had a sufficient number of warm-weather colonists from below the Mason-Dixon Line.

With the election of Lincoln, however, dissension spread over Maryland, and the Ridgelys found that they had to be constantly defending their politics. "Even as a child," Harry wrote later, "I greatly disliked heated discussions between members of the family and their friends, and hardly a day passed that I did not hear one or more such during which the parties thereto frequently lost their tempers and ended, some of them, by not speaking to each other." The future peacemaker may have already spied his role.

Right at the war's end, in 1865, White's mother married Dr. Thomas H. Buckler, a distinguished physician who had treated President Buchanan, Chief Justice Taney, and General Lee. He shared his wife's violent Confederate sympathies, and they agreed to move to Paris, where he had engaged in medical research as a young man. Harry was educated entirely by tutors, even giving up the prospect of Cambridge University because of ill health when he was nineteen. Mrs. Buckler, however, saw to it that his education was not neglected. She was a strong-minded woman, plain, forceful, indifferent to dress and society, intensely religious, and a strict disciplinarian. She insisted that her sons maintain regular hours, keep to their books, and learn the chief modern tongues. Harry grew up as a rarity in Parisian society, a man of the world without any of its vices.

For Mrs. Buckler had no objection to her sons, immunized from temptation, going into the "great world," and Harry attended balls and dinners, went to the theatre and opera, and rode regularly in the Bois de Boulogne. In 1870 the family abandoned a beleaguered Paris to settle in London, and for almost a decade Harry did nothing but ride, hunt, pay weekend visits, and generally indulge a strong taste for a fashionable life of sport and leisure. Just why the stern and puritanical Mrs. Buckler approved of such an existence we don't know. She may have thought it the best way to build up his health, which had once been a cause of anxiety. She may have believed that so long as a man's faith and morals were in good repair, a career was superfluous. Or she may have even agreed with Harry's own later evaluation of this period of his life: "The nine winters of fox hunting were the best preparation that I could have had for the twenty-one years of diplomacy of which I was subsequently (though I little knew it at the time) to have experience in England; not only because of the opportunities for acquiring a thorough knowledge of the different classes, but of meeting many of the leading men of the period, and also those who became more or less prominent, politically or otherwise, during the years which were to follow."

I am not so sure about the different classes, but there can be no doubt about the leading men. A handsome and agreeable unattached young man of ample means, who excelled at all popular sports, was welcome, although American, at the very grandest country houses, and England was still ruled by the men who owned or leased them. The franchise had been extended, it was true, and something was beginning to be done about the dismal condition of the poor, but the old aristocracy, unlike that of France, had shown itself adaptable to a capitalist world, both in its marriages and its investments. Society was fluid, though money was the ticket. If a new lord had to give up his seat in the Commons, he could rest assured that he was leaving plenty of friends in the lower house.

One wonders, however, if Harry, despite his valuable training in pursuit of the fox, would have found his way into diplomacy without the prodding of the beautiful, brilliant, and ambitious Margaret Rutherfurd, whom he met on one of his now frequent visits to his native land and whom he married in 1879. The Rutherfurds, a rich old New York family descended from a "signer," had no patience with European notions of a *désoeuvré* society. Margaret's father, Lewis Morris Rutherfurd, was an astronomer of note, and she soon, according to Harry, "began to talk to me about doing something useful in the world, a matter which we thereupon began to discuss from time to time." They decided upon diplomacy, an obvious enough choice in view of Harry's means, background, and languages, and he began to study for his new career and knock on government doors in Washington. It was four years, however, before he received his first appointment, as secretary of legation in Vienna, in 1884. How he learned of it, as described by his biographer, Allan Nevins, is illuminating, both as to his ultimate value to the foreign service and his difficulties with American politicians.

A few weeks later White, having rejoined his wife in Europe, was paying a visit to Ferdinand Rothschild's new house at Waddesdon Manor, in Buckinghamshire, where a great housewarming had been arranged. The guests included the Prince of Wales, later Edward VII, the Duchess of Manchester, and Lady Kildar, later the Duchess of Leinster. White and other guests, one afternoon when fireworks had been announced, played tennis on the lawn till nearly eight o'clock; when they retired to dress for dinner there had been no apparent preparation for the coming display; but happening to look out of the window of his room, White suddenly saw a perfect army of workmen creeping out of the bushes in all directions, and beginning to erect frameworks for the various set pieces. They had been kept in hiding in the shrubberies since lunchtime in order to do their work inconspicuously and without delay. At this houseparty a telegram was handed him from Alphonso Taft, the American minister to Austria.

Harry was not long in Vienna. He was soon called to the more important post of second secretary to the embassy in London, where in a year's time he was promoted to first secretary. He served there until 1892, under James Russell Lowell, Edward Phelps, and Robert Todd Lincoln, and it was widely recognized that he ably and tactfully ran the embassy for these ministers. They relied heavily and not in vain on his long experience with British society. He and Margaret were the only American members of the "Gang" or "Souls," a super-select group thus described by Nevins:

They were made interesting by their brilliant social gifts and by the breadth of their interests; sports, games, literature, art, philosophy, politics, religion were all open for discussion at their gatherings. They had wealth, beauty, intellect and culture at their command. Among them were hostesses who owned some of the most beautiful country houses in England, and at Panshanger, Ashridge, Wilton and Taplow these congenial spirits would assemble for weekends. . . . Their origin may be traced in part to the determination of a few people closely connected with politics not to let the acrimony of the Home Rule controversy spoil their social intercourse.

And what did Harry White, who was neither witty nor a brilliant talker, nor even, to tell the truth, a man of very deep cultivation, contribute to this "gang"? "I really think it was his goodness," Lord

Robert Cecil suggested. "He never said an ill-natured or bitter thing in his life. He never claimed anything as his due. If there was a dull or disagreeable duty to be done, Harry took it on. Every lame dog naturally turned to him for help. To say he was unselfish is inadequate. He lived to increase the happiness of others."

Not everyone saw Harry that way. He presented a very different picture to the jealous eyes of Daniel Lamont, who in 1892 was the newly designated secretary of war for the reelected Grover Cleveland. On a visit to London, while White had been engrossed in legation work owing to the absence of Lincoln, Lamont was incensed by the first secretary's failure to call on him, and White spent the next four years without a post.

There could be no greater tribute to his abilities, however, than the State Department's continuing to make use of them even while he was out of favor with the administration. Secretary of State Richard Olney sent him without title or salary to London to be an unofficial assistant in the tricky arbitration of the boundary dispute between Venezuela and British Guiana which threatened to erupt into war, and one that would involve the United States, President Cleveland having invoked the Monroe Doctrine. Nevins describes how White operated:

Within ten days after he landed in England on June 3rd, White had seen every English leader important for his purposes, without making any special appointments, at dinners or receptions. He had lunched with Arthur Balfour, and had taken him down to his country place for the weekend; he had spent a second weekend at a country place where H. H. Asquith was present; he had talked with Lord Rothschild, a leader of great financial interests, and Sir William Harcourt, the head of the opposition, and Lord Salisbury, the prime minister, had asked him down to Hatfield for a day. White was thus able to furnish our government expert reports on the situation.

In the subsequent administrations of McKinley and of White's close friend, Theodore Roosevelt, White's services were again made full use of. In 1897 he returned to the London embassy under John Hay, where he remained until 1904, when he was appointed ambassador to Italy. While in that post he represented the United States at the Algeciras Conference in Morocco, which prevented a near war between France and Germany. In 1907 he went as ambassador to France, where his career was terminated in 1909 by Roosevelt's successor, Taft.

Senator Henry Cabot Lodge of Massachusetts, another of White's close friends, wrote him about what had happened:

You have discovered the secret of your retirement, which I shrink from explaining, as did Root [Elihu Root], it seems so inconceivable. The exact story is this. It seems that when Taft went abroad on his wedding journey some twenty-five years ago, and you having been with his father [Alphonso Taft in Vienna], he went to call upon you. He asked for you to procure for him tickets to the House of Commons. You said that you had none, or could not obtain them, and sent him tickets of admission to the royal mews. That is his whole story. He told it to Roosevelt, then to me, then to Root and one night at a party to Constance [Lodge's daughter]. That was in December, and in each and every case he said: "He made me very angry at the time. Now I don't care and I am going to keep him." . . . . When he reached home in March the President became suspicious that all was not well, and when I saw him I saw the change. Then Aldrich [Nelson Aldrich] and Root took hold, most earnestly. But it was in vain, and he finally told Root decisively that you were to go in January.

On such threads hang the fate of our diplomats! The jealousy aroused in rural congressmen by the type of suave, sophisticated legate, always dropping titles, is understandable, and was not unjustified with some of White's successors. But Harry himself was *sui generis*.

One last job, the biggest of all if not the most successful (through no fault of his own), remained. In 1918 President Wilson appointed White one of the four American Peace Commissioners to negotiate what would become known as the Treaty of Versailles. The other three were fairly obvious choices: Robert Lansing, secretary of state; Colonel Edward House, Wilson's closest adviser and (many thought) his *éminence grise*; and General Tasker Bliss, the inevitable military man. But the selection of White was far from indicated. It was incumbent upon a Democratic President to appoint a Republican to the commission if he ever hoped to see his treaty ratified, and this need was hardly met, in the eyes of elected politicians, by the choice of a gentleman diplomat who had never run for office and whose contributions to the party were at the most financial. Indeed, it could have been taken by some of the Old Guard as a slap in the face.

No one was more aware of this than White himself. Still, it was hardly a job an old public servant could turn down, and, given Wilson's stubborn and imperious temper, the next choice might well have been worse. What White determined to do was to get in touch and stay in touch with the Republican leaders and try to persuade them that their wishes would not be ignored. He went to see the dying Theodore Roosevelt and took notes on his belief in a league of nations; he did the same with Elihu Root. His greatest and most prolonged effort was with Lodge who, he rightly saw, would be the key in the Senate to the ratification of any treaty and whose goodwill the arrogant Wilson, carried away by the cheers of a welcoming Europe, had fatally ignored. Lodge was willing to listen to his old friend Harry, but he was dead set against the idea of a league of nations, at least until well after any treaty had been agreed upon, and was determined to kill any covenant to the treaty calling for such a league. He was also in favor of harsh and crippling reparations to be imposed on the defeated enemy.

White himself was not initially convinced of the need for the league, but he became so in the bitter, bickering months in Paris. He wrote tirelessly to Lodge, but to little avail. In March of 1919 the old peacemaker made a last desperate plea to his unconvinced friend.

In view of the fact that more than seven million, two hundred and forty-odd thousand men have been killed in this war; that five million more men have been entirely incapacitated for any sort of usefulness during the rest of their lives, either by blindness or the loss of both arms or legs or one of the innumerable reasons which you can imagine, I cannot but feel that a strenuous effort must be made to try to prevent a return to the barbarous methods hitherto prevailing, which will, of course, be even more barbarous hereafter in view of the constant scientific improvements in weapons for the destruction of human life.

Alas! Lodge stuck to his attitude that Wilson had agreed to a treaty that no one respected in return for a league that nobody wanted. The treaty and the covenant were rejected by the Senate, and all Wilson's work went up in smoke. It was one of the wonderful qualities in Harry White that he was able to keep his friendship with Cabot Lodge intact. But then he never gave up hope that with patience and hard work the most seemingly irreconcilable differences of opinion could be worked out. Who knew? The time might come for another league. It was a pity that he and Cabot and Woodrow couldn't go fox hunting together.

Harry's great gift to the republic was his understanding of the uses of power. He had recognized power when he had seen his grandfather box the ears of a slave. He had seen it in English peers, in Roman cardinals, in American Presidents and congressmen. He knew there was no point in lamenting the misuse of power; one might as well lament a thunderstorm. The only point of a useful diplomatic life was to create shelters from it. Harry did not feel personally offended, either when he was dismissed from his post because of an oversensitive politician or when the treaty for which he had labored was sacrificed to the conflict between an arrogant President and an egotistical senator. Those things were the given situation, as his friend Henry James would put it, the *donnée*. They were one's job.

Gertrude Whitney

Gertrude Vanderbilt Whitney (*left*) and Adele Sloane Burden
in fancy dress.

I N 1893, when Gertrude, daughter of Cornelius II and Alice, was eighteen, she started a history of her life with this episode: "One of the first things I remember was how I longed to be a boy. I was four years old when, unable to resist the temptation longer, I secreted myself in my mother's room and proceeded to cut off my curls."

Her life from the beginning had been fraught with ambiguities. Her parents, as we have seen, combined an almost ludicrously ostentatious train of existence with the driest and strictest Puritan morality. Life around her was viewed in a frame of gold, yet nothing was supposed to count like true love. Art was something one's decorator bought abroad; any craving to create it was at best a harmless urge, at worst a distraction from the main job of being Papa's daughter. True love came with marriage, and nice young men liked beautiful girls, and Gertrude, bonily thin and large of feature, was certainly not that. But mightn't she be? She had fine green eyes, and both men and women looked at her. Which did she like best?

Her first cousin, Consuelo, two years her junior, daughter of her uncle, William K., was an undoubted beauty, but was that the real point? "Gertrude and I were *heiresses,*" Consuelo recalled, in a conversation I had with her in her old age. "There seemed never to have been a time when this was not made entirely clear."

Gertrude's history continues: "When I was eleven I knew perfectly that my father was talked of all over, that his name was known throughout the world, that I, simply because I was his daughter, would be talked about when I grew up, and that there were lots of things I could not do simply because I was Miss Vanderbilt. At first I felt as if I could not stand this."

But in time, according to her "history," she decided that God would not have placed her where she was without the strength to see it through, and she resolved to resign herself to her fate, adding with a touch of defiance: "For let me tell you I had friends in spite of the terrible obstacle which stood in our way. There were girls who liked me for myself, I know it. I was not altogether unlovable, I think."

One of these was certainly Esther Hunt, daughter of the architect, whose violent crush on Gertrude was in some part returned. Alice Vanderbilt, who in Gertrude's phrase always found dignity a "prime factor" in life, did not at all approve of the unrestrained and gushing Esther. Indeed any mother, at least of that day, would have been disgusted by a girlfriend of her daughter who wrote: "Your mouth, Gertrude, your mouth someday will drive me crazy. I kiss it softly at first, perhaps shortly too, then for longer, then somehow I want you all, entirely and almost I care not if I hurt you," particularly had she seen Gertrude's entry in her journal that one of the few thrills of her life had been "when Esther kissed me."

Gertrude appears also to have had some feeling for an English teacher at the Brearley School, a Miss Winsor, to whom she wrote, but did not send, one of her early imaginary epistles. "You will be very surprised to get this long letter from me, no doubt," she began, and went on to assert that however low an opinion Miss Winsor might have of the writer's talents in rhetoric class, she, Gertrude, though a person who usually neither aired her opinions nor approved of those who did, still wanted Miss Winsor to know that "you are to me as few others and as no one at school." And then she composed Miss Winsor's surprised response: "I take as conclusion to your letter that you would like to know me better, and I can say that I have often thought, but especially in reading certain of your compositions, that I would like to know *you* better."

Gertrude's initial "history" ran only to forty-nine pages, but the inner need that produced it was never satiated, and all her life long she was to make and keep records of her reactions to experience, so that at her death the bulk was comparable, quantitatively, to that of some professional writers. There are journals; drafts of letters later sent; imaginary letters with imagined replies; records of dreams, conversations, and fantasies; seatings for dinner parties; anticipations of future events with later accounts of what actually happened; short stories, plays, and ultimately whole novels—a remarkable medley of fact and fiction, expressing the writer's compulsion to dramatize herself, to berate herself, to romanticize herself, to make some sense out of the comedy or tragedy or simple bathos of being Gertrude Vanderbilt.

The young men to whom, as a debutante, she was now constantly introduced soon relegated Esther and Miss Winsor to secondary status. In 1894 she was writing: "To make a man feel for me, thrill for me, long for me, care for a little while once for me, this in my present mood seems happiness."

But there was always the money. Only the year before, she had made this gloomy prognostication: "I look into the future and imagine I see myself, grown up and out. I meet a man. I love him. He is attentive to me for my money. He proposes, makes me believe he loves me. I accept, since I love him. We are married. Now, since the money is secure, he shows me that he does not love me. I love him still and am wretchedly unhappy. We lead separate lives, he going his way, I mine. And thus we grow old."

In the London season of 1894 Gertrude, traveling with her family, met Lord Garwick, heir of the earl of Mar, an amiable young man whose establishment stood in sore need of American capital and who showed his seriousness of purpose by inviting Gertrude and her parents to have lunch with his. Gertrude jotted down in her journal a prediction of what the party and her hosts would be like: "The countess of Mar—an elderly lady with gray hair, a black silk dress, a little lace cap on her head, dignified yet small. The earl of Mar—a tall oldish man, slightly bent with age, having old-fashioned manners. Piercing eyes that seem to see into you." The reality was close to her picture with some exceptions, duly recorded. "Though Lady Mar had on the black silk dress I felt sure she would," she was younger looking than Gertrude had imagined, and Lord Mar's eye proved not to be piercing.

Cornelius and Alice apparently agreed with their daughter that Garwick was not for her, and the three seem to have been congenial in their shared amusement over the episode, but such unanimity was not always the case. Alice's disapproval of one of Gertrude's New York beaux produced this impassioned entry: "I shall put it down in black and white or die—I hate her. Who? My mother. Yes, ha ha, I have never allowed myself to say it, to think it scarcely before." But she soon got over the tantrum, and apparently the beau as well; the scene was set for Harry Payne Whitney. She had not despaired, she wrote to herself, of the possibility "that anyone in all the world would not care for the money but would care as much as his life for me."

Harry, young, handsome, charming, well liked by her family and much richer than she, certainly did not care for her money and may have cared for her as much as he cared for his life. But how much did he care for that? With the ability to do surpassingly well all the things that he wanted to do, particularly in polo and horse racing, he was inclined to take life as it very agreeably came to him and was the last person to understand the restless, moody, and talented young woman with whom he had fallen in love.

New York society in the nineties may have been heavily commercial in its makeup and interests—the Four Hundred, according to Mrs. Winthrop Chanler, would have fled in a body from "a painter, a musician or a clever Frenchman"—but it was also naïvely romantic. It utterly repudiated the European tradition that a young man starting out in life had every right to expect a dower with his bride. What it *should* have been protecting its daughters from, considering the era and milieu, was not the man who expected a dower with the woman he loved, but the man who was interested *only* in the dower, the lazy worldling who sought to be supported in style while he yachted or hunted, or simply gambled and drank. It is difficult not to suspect, in view of Gertrude's constantly expressed apprehension of mercenary suitors, that one of Harry's strong attractions was the fortune that exempted him from suspicion.

Of course it may have worked both ways. Harry, too, may have been afraid of gold diggers, so that in one sense of the term they were both married for their money. Gertrude would have been better off with a man like Willard Straight, who married Harry's sister Dorothy. Brilliant and self-made, a promising partner in Morgan Grenfell, Willard might, with the added push of a fortune behind him, have carried his wife to the top of any world they cared to conquer. No one could have foreseen that he would die young in the flu epidemic. Yet such was the blind fear of fortune hunters that as shrewd a man as E. H. Harriman had broken up an incipient engagement between Straight and his daughter Mary. The heiresses had little chance.

If the Vanderbilts were delighted with the match, Harry's mother, Flora Payne Whitney, who had died three years previously, might have been less so. She had a deeper sense of the kind of girl her charming but epicurean son needed, and on her deathbed she had extracted his promise that he would offer his hand to Gertrude's first cousin, Adele Sloane. Flora may have been shrewd in her choice if not her method. Adele was bright, pretty, and full of the love of life. She shared Harry's passion for horses and hunting, but she had also a deeply serious side and might have been just the partner he needed to guide him into a career other than horse breeding and racing. But her discovery of the deathbed promise and her immediate need to release Harry from any possible obligation to her created an awkwardness that was probably fatal to any further development of romance. Poor Mrs. Whitney had created a fatal block to her posthumous project.

There is a moving entry in Gertrude's journal in 1898, two years after the wedding, a period long enough for her to have discovered that her new life was a disappointing duplicate of her old, when she spies the possibility of a truer salvation: "The house I had stepped into after my marriage was furnished complete and full. Beautiful paintings hung on the walls. Beautiful Renaissance tapestries. Furniture of all the Louis. It was the same atmosphere in which I had been brought up, the very same surroundings. Just as physically I had moved some fifty feet from my father's house into my husband's, so I had moved some fifty feet in feeling, environment, and period. No more than that, and it was a very big jump for me when I began to realize the possibilities of something new in art. . . ."

She was now sculpting seriously, realizing an early dream in which she had been in a cellar, modeling the figure of a man. One feels it was a nude, a harbinger of all the large male figures she would create, merging her artistic and romantic needs. It was unfortunate that her first teacher should have been Hendrik Christian Andersen (a distant relative of the writer of children's tales), the strapping young Scandinavian artist who had aroused such strong homoerotic feelings in the great novelist Henry James. The latter's letters to him would end with rhapsodic signatures like "your poor old helpless far off but all devoted HJ, who seems condemned almost and never to be near you, yet who, if he were, would lay upon you a pair of hands soothing, sustaining, positively healing in the quality of their pressure." But James's heart could never cloud his eye when it was a question of art appreciation, and he could not blind himself to the empty monumentality of the sculptor's work, some of which briefly escaped oblivion only to adorn the pompous public buildings of Mussolini's Rome. All James could do was try to persuade his young friend at least to be practical. "What American community," he implored him, "is going to want to pay for thirty and forty stark-naked men and women, of whatever beauty, and lifted into the raw light of one of their public places?" He begged him "to stop your multiplication of unsaleable nakedness for a while and hurl yourself into the production of the interesting, the charming, the vendible, the *placeable* small thing."

The postscript on an Andersen letter to Gertrude from England, where he had been visiting the master, reads, "I have talked so much to Henry James about you who is so very much in sympathy with your work." It is a pity that Gertrude did not live near James. Had she shown him her work she might have received and even taken the advice that he wasted upon the stubbornly obsessed Scandinavian. For the small things that she was later to do, statuettes of daughters and nieces, for example, have charm and grace, while her public monuments disappoint with their impersonality. As her biographer, B. H. Friedman, has said: "We miss what exists typically in the sketches and studies for these works (and also typically in the best of her journals and letters)—intimacy, immediacy, tenderness of touch—qualities lacking in almost all large-scale public sculpture which, by definition, cannot be intimate and which generally demands the surrender of the artist's own hands to those of artisans. Too often Gertrude betrays her intimate talent in the pursuit of public commissions."

As her work progressed, her relationship with Harry deteriorated. Their friends and interests were now too different. Soon there would be other women for him, and later, other men for her. But neither could ever really accept the loss of their old love. He resented her least affair; she resented his serious ones. She was troubled by his drinking and began to keep a wary eye on her own. When Harry put on weight, she described him in her journal as "Fatty," though the word was later crossed out and "Harry" written in above. She did not like what she felt that she was becoming. In 1901 she wrote, "How I hate myself tonight and all my weaknesses and follies and how I should love to change places with *anybody*."

There seems never to have been a question of divorce between them. They not only liked and respected each other; they were deeply committed to their three children. Gertrude once summed up her husband as "quick, bright and good company," with a brain for which discipline might have done wonders. But life, she sorrowfully added, had given him all he asked for from the beginning. The miracle, to her, was that he retained any strength at all.

With middle age Gertrude's inner life, the one expressed in her journals, and her outer ones, those of the sculptor, the art collector, the hostess, the wife and mother, the lover and would-be lover, began to spill out of their categories, so that the reader of her papers is less and less sure which passage is fact and which fiction. Some of her fantasies read like dime novels. On one of her manys trips to Europe, in Sicily, she thought of herself as "a woman of fire and of passion with a thousand loves in my heart and a million lovers in my train. I imagined myself with an inexhaustible passion. I walked one night in a garden of orange blossoms and longed with a deadly longing for the arms of my lover." And in that garden she meets a savage man. "I fainted into his arms and he took me as savage men take their women, and I was happy."

Yet more and more, at least to the eyes of the world, Gertrude assumed the role of the reserved and self-assured great lady, empha- sized by her tall, thin, sinewy figure, her rapid, high-heeled stride, her green stare, and the craggy, impressive features of her pale counte- nance. But one might also have seen her, in 1914, at a charity ball, dancing for an Oriental tableau in flowing veils with nine macaws. She may have been amused to reflect how little the woman in the garden fainting into the arms of the savage was detectable in the visitor to the Belmont racetrack or Bailey's Beach. Like an actress in repertoire who is Juliet one night and Lady Macbeth the next, she may have solved what today might be called her identity crisis by rotating her different images. But there may be a danger to the artist in such games. Making a work of art of oneself can detract from the making of art.

Her love affairs seem never to have brought her what she had sought from the "savage man." As B. H. Friedman puts it, they appear to have been largely the product of loneliness, expressed as much in the fantasies of her autocommunications as in bed. And she could never get over her failure to hold Harry's love. In 1905, ill and apprehensive of dying, she wrote him a "last" letter, never of course sent, in which she professed to understand his unfaithfulness, which he could not help,

89

and to speculate that her own demise might be the best solution to her greediness for a love that he could not provide. And she once "accidentally" left her correspondence with a lover where Harry found and read it, promoting a scene in the drama of which she may have hoped to rekindle some embers of his old passion.

In 1906, with recovered health, Gertrude sounded a more positive note in her journal:

"Tomorrow I shall go to the studio. I shall go early and lunch there and then Mac [the model] will come and his beautiful bare body will be more beautiful than ever, and I will look at him and be glad that I am alive and that my heart beats, now quickly, now slowly, and there will be symmetry of lines that will call to my soul, and those dormant things in my mind will awake and I will long with a terrible pain to express them."

She now embarked on the career for which she will always be remembered: that of a patron of American art. In 1908 she bought paintings by Henri, Luks, and Shinn at a show at the Macbeth Gallery. John Sloan's diary records: "All the sales went to three buyers. Mrs. Harry Payne Whitney, the rich sculptress—at least she has a fine studio for the purpose—bought four."

Her taste, as manifested in a lifetime of collecting, was primarily for American realists: such painters as those mentioned above and such sculptors as Jo Davidson and Mahonri Young. She was much less interested in Cubism and abstract painting and the host of American artists who followed the school of Picasso and Matisse. But the vital part that she played in the history of native art is not measured in what she bought, but in all she did for artists in the Whitney Studio, where their works were exhibited and ultimately in the Whitney Museum of American Art. If her taste and that of her appointed director, Juliana Force, may have limited the development of the museum's collection in its early years, Gertrude had nonetheless established a vital and permanent cultural institution which would vastly enlarge its scope in the fullness of time.

A sad, late drama in Gertrude's life was the custody trial over her brother Reginald's daughter, Gloria, in 1934. Gertrude, who had had the little girl for long visits in New York and Long Island while her beautiful young widowed sister-in-law disported herself on the French Riviera with money taken from the child's maintenance fund, was persuaded at last that her niece should be formally removed from her mother's tutelage. A bitter trial ensued in which much scandalous evidence of heavy drinking, fornication, and lesbianism was introduced to challenge Mrs. Vanderbilt's parental fitness, and Gertrude at length won a Pyrrhic victory, receiving custody of the child but ultimately losing her affection.

Why did she do it? Suppose she had simply said to her pleasure-loving but essentially harmless sister-in-law: "Gloria, my dear, it strikes my you've been looking a bit run down lately. Why don't you let me lease a villa for you in Nice for the winter and pick up the tab for your expenses? I know how you hate to be away from little Gloria, but don't you think she's really better off at school on Long Island? I'll be glad to take care of her, and she'll be near little cousins her own age. And there'll be a cottage on the place for you to have her with you any time you care to come, which I hope will be very often."

I don't think many people who remember the principals of that sorry lawsuit would doubt that such an offer would have been rapidly accepted. It would have cost Gertrude far less than her legal expenses, and it would have spared the child the trauma of the trial. But instead Gertrude elected to put the young widow in a position so grossly humiliating that she had no choice but to fight back.

Gertrude was also taking grave risks. What about her own life? Friedman claims her discretion had been so great that the older Gloria's counsel never picked up the scent, but Barbara Goldsmith, author of *Little Gloria, Happy at Last,* a deeply researched study of the trial, has shown that they had indeed picked it up and only agreed to drop it when threatened by Gertrude's lawyers with further and even more scandalous revelations about the child's mother.

Was it simply, then, the arrogance of great wealth that caused Gertrude's haughty refusal to stoop to persuasion and her resolution to use the mailed fist to squash the woman who had captured her alcoholic brother, neglected his child, and squandered his money? In part. People raised as Gertrude had been were not disposed to plead when they could have their way without it. Her father had never forgiven his eldest son, Cornelius III, for marrying what he had deemed a frivolous woman. But I think there was more to it than that.

I think that what Gertrude could not tolerate in her sister-in-law was the latter's open abandonment of the conventions and moral obligations that Gertrude herself had so scrupulously and painfully observed all her life. Gertrude had found marriage and children confining, and the society into which she had been born even more so, but she had always maintained its forms. She and Harry had kept their differences and infidelities to themselves. They had entertained and traveled together; he went to her art shows and she to his races. If she left her children, even when they were very young, for months at a time when she went abroad, they were always well looked after and constantly written to. The other side of her life, even when she may have considered it the more important one, was confined to the studio, to discreet assignations, to her journals. To one who had subjected herself to such rigors, the looseness of Gloria's festive life must have been singularly disgusting. And nothing begets cruelty like disgust. To Gertrude the difference between a lady and a tramp was that the lady must conceal the tramp in her.

Her attitude may have been expressed in an interchange at the trial between her and Nathan Burkan, Gloria's lawyer. The latter was trying to show Gertrude's unfitness as guardian of the child on the ground that she had worked with nude male models. Gertrude explained that they had always worn a fig leaf.

"After you completed the work of designing, you tore off the fig leaf, is that it?" Burkan demanded.

"Off the statue I did," Gertrude replied. "I did not on the model."

FLORENCE ADELE
SLOANE

Adele and "J" Burden (with George Vanderbilt and St. Bernard)
on their honeymoon at Biltmore.

ANOTHER GRANDDAUGHTER of William Henry Vanderbilt, Adele Sloane, was almost as passionate a journalist as Gertrude. The diary that she kept from 1891, when she was eighteen, to the time of her marriage to James A. Burden three years later, is more romantic, more accepting of the good things in life than that of her devoted cousin and almost exact contemporary. Adele loved the outdoors of the Berkshires, where her parents had erected the vast shingle pile called Elm Court; she would ride across country as much as twenty miles a day. In Europe she could enjoy acres of beautiful pictures and sculptures without the pang of needing to create one herself. And in New York and on visits to uncles and aunts in Newport, she found the dinners and dances altogether delightful. Turning the pages of her lively diary we see her with an amiable, chattering flock of cousins, moving from Lenox to the Adirondacks to Boston's North Shore, and up to Bar Harbor in Maine or down to Asheville in North Carolina. We see them cantering through the hills of western Massachusetts, riding a buckboard on the trails of Mount Desert Island, watching the sunset from the deck of a steam yacht or from the rear porch of a private railway car. The sight of the privileged classes enjoying their privileges is, in the words of the playwright Philip Barry, apt to be a pretty one.

Adele does not seem to have been gnawed by the fear of being married for her money. It is even possible that she did not, like Consuelo and Gertrude, consider herself an heiress, a technical term in that opulent era. Her mother had been one, of course; she had received ten million under William Henry's will. But she had four children and a husband with a considerably smaller fortune. One of Sloane's grandsons had spied a casual memo on the old man's desk in which he reminded himself to pay back a million dollars which he had borrowed from "EVS" (his wife). In the society in which the Sloanes moved many of their friends were as rich as they, and some (though by no means all) of Adele's beaux had prospects equal to her own. As most people tend to look up rather than down the social ladder in appraising their means, it was perfectly feasible for Adele to consider herself only moderately well off. She was spared, therefore, the disadvantage of suffering either the uneasiness, in Gertrude's case, or the "guileless confidence," in the case of Gwen Van Osburgh in Edith Wharton's *The House of Mirth*, "of a young girl who has always been told that there is no one richer than her father." But where Adele did stand out a bit from other debutantes of her day—a tribute perhaps to her unusual vivacity and charm—was in having her own listing in the Four Hundred (actually three) that Ward McAllister had the fatuity to publish in 1892.

Here is how Adele saw herself at nineteen:

I have an easy natural figure, because I have never worn anything tight or never in the least squeezed myself. I have a moderately small foot, and I suppose a very well-shaped leg; only no one ever sees that. . . . My eyes are black and my eyelashes long and my eyebrows thick. My hair is dark brown and brushed back off my forehead, with sometimes a little curl in the middle, and always done in a Psyche knot in the back. I suppose I am moderately graceful and perhaps very much so on horseback; at least, so people tell me. But after this truthful picture I certainly cannot understand how people can look at me and tell me that I am beautiful.

William Douglas Sloane, whose family carpet business was well looked after by his brothers, had plenty of time to travel, and he was determined that his three daughters should grow up cultivated women, which in his day meant learning French, Italian, and German, and visiting the museums and cathedrals of old Europe. Adele attended a small private girls' school in New York from which she could be plucked at any time for a trip abroad. She was taught to play the piano and to recite poetry, but economics and science were no more required than cooking. A girl was brought up to marry, to supervise a household, and to entertain.

Emily Vanderbilt Sloane, Adele's mother, was quite the opposite of her sister-in-law Alva. She had no wish to marry her daughters to dukes or even to millionaires. It was nice, of course, if a prospective son-in-law had some money of his own, for she could not wholly escape the universal fear of the fortune hunter, but the primary thing that she and her husband sought was character. When Adele fell in love with Gifford Pinchot, the brilliant young architect of George Vanderbilt's forestry plan at Biltmore, Emily was only too happy to invite him to Elm Court, but Pinchot, eight years older than his boss's pretty niece, had already engaged his affections elsewhere, and however intrigued by his evident conquest, he was too kind to trifle with her feelings.

Adele got over him, but not without considerable pain. "I am sure it will be a horrible winter for me," she wrote in her diary when she learned he was to be in New York, "always in a fear of excitement at a dance, always wondering if he will talk to me. And how often he will hurt me through and through! I believe the more he hurts me, the more I will love him." She even began to reassess her life, which she now considered a "horrible waste." "I ought to have some work to do, some hard work, that would take my time and mind and everything else."

Fortunately there were distractions, and the image of Pinchot receded. It may have been a pity that things did not work out between the two, as she would have been a strong partner for him in his long and useful life. Another admirer did not meet with the same parental approval. When Creighton Webb, a forty-year-old roué and the bachelor brother of Adele's Uncle Seward, turned his ogling attentions in her direction, her mother informed her roundly that she would rather see her in her coffin than married to such a man. So that was that.

And then James A. Burden, Jr., made his first appearance in Adele's life. It was almost too much of a good thing. He was handsome, clean-cut, athletic, and rich, a Harvard man whose family, residents of Fifth Avenue and Newport, were known to the Sloanes and whose grandfather had been Henry Burden, the ironmaster of Troy. Adele, in her old age, describing to me how she and "J" had become engaged on a bench in Bryant Park after a matinée of *Tristan und Isolde* and gone to her parents' house to tell them, confessed to a feeling of letdown when both the latter rose to exclaim, "We couldn't be more pleased!" Might not the course of her love have been too smooth to be quite true?

She was to have, however, between the beginning of her interest in J and his ultimate declaration, a tempestuous fling at romance with a suitor who was quite charmingly ineligible. Frederick O. Beach was a dashing man-about-town, of no recorded means or employment but with many swanky friends, a flowing black mustache, and a steady hand for driving a coach-and-four. He was fifteen years older than Adele and a good deal more sophisticated than any of her other beaux except Webb. The only likeness that I have been able to discover of him shows him on top of a coach in a gray top hat, reins in hand, the "whip" on the road from Tuxedo to Nyack. It seems in character.

Adele met Beach at a dinner party in Newport in the summer of 1893, and they found themselves immediately congenial. He offered to teach her coaching, and she invited him to visit her at Elm Court the following month. Things went very fast after that, as her diary shows: ". . . we managed to be outdoors most of the time. In the morning we went in the brake, and he taught me a lot of things in driving. I am crazy about it and go out every morning. Mr. Beach was very encouraging and told me he was sure I would drive perfectly. . . . I do not know how much I will end in liking Mr. Beach, if the liking keeps on increasing at the rate it is now. I have never had a more glorious ride. We went up on the top of the mountain, and the view—well, one can't explain impossible things."

The rules of chaperonage in the nineties are difficult to understand. A young lady could not go alone to the theatre with a gentleman unless they were engaged, yet she could ride out all day with him across the countryside, and they could tether their horses and sit down together on some lonely hilltop and contemplate the view to their hearts' content. Hadn't their elders read *Madame Bovary*? Perhaps not. Or was the fresh air of the out-of-doors supposed to be more conducive to virtue than the greasepaint of the theatre? At any rate Beach must have been sufficiently encouraged by what happened on their ride to propose to her three days later. At least that is how I interpret the following passage:

I could not write yesterday on my twentieth birthday, but it will be a day I will not soon forget. I think if I took all the pain I have ever suffered in my life and crowded it all into four hours, it would just about equal what I suffered yesterday from twelve o'clock until four. It was exquisite intense pain that was impossible to bear. I do not know what got into me. The way he calls me "dear child"; I can hear it over and over again. If I married him, would he make me happy? But no, I must not think of that; it is an absolute impossibility.

Why? The letter that Beach wrote her subsequently, lovingly transcribed in her journal, is almost convincingly intense: "You have stirred to the bottom a desire to be worthy of you. O, I love you so! As you say, it has been only a short time, and yet I love you better than anything in the world and would give up everything in it for you. If you only knew how lonely and sad my life is!" It does not strike one as the letter of a cynical fortune hunter, and Beach had some respectable friends who were willing to vouch for him, including two of Adele's Vanderbilt uncles. But he was a lot older, and that seemed to affect Adele, who wrote: "He has had his life too long to enter into mine," and he had no prospects and the reputation of being a womanizer, though just what that term meant to the Sloanes is not clear.

Adele met him again at a house party at Shelburne Farms given by her Aunt Lila and Uncle Seward Webb. But by this time they were both miserable.

I feel too horribly blue to write any of the things he said to me. I am tired and lonely today. It was a fearful strain on me yesterday, trying to keep up all the time. We took a long walk together in the morning and a three-hour ride in the afternoon. Then I sat next to him at dinner, and that was the hardest of all. It choked me to swallow, and about every five or ten minutes his eyes would all fill up with tears, and he couldn't look up because it seemed as if everyone at the table was looking at us. I thought the meal would never finish; then the frightful goodbye with everyone around, and I knew that he would break down unless I could be supernaturally cheerful. It is almost like a nightmare now. Everyone in this houseparty thinks we are in love with each other. I don't know what Mamma will say when she hears it, and I don't know what I am going to say to her. I wish the whole thing was over and done with or that it had never been. No, I don't either; I don't know what I wish, excepting that I might stop thinking.

A month later, however, at Uncle George's at Biltmore, she more resolutely faced her own involvement: "The only man I am in love with is Mr. Beach. There are probably ninety-eight reasons why I should not marry him, and two reasons why I should—the first that he is desperately in love with me, and the second that I care very much for him. I have not the slightest idea if it will ever come to anything. My family certainly do not want it. I think Mamma would like me to marry J Burden. As he is not in love with me, and I not the least in love with him, this is rather a useless wish."

The Sloanes now had to be told of the situation, and Emily did what mothers of her class and period did: she planned a trip to Europe to get her daughter away from the undesirable Beach. The yacht *Roxanna* was chartered for a Mediterranean cruise. "I shall certainly not go to any place where you would meet Mr. Beach," Emily told her daughter. "If he is in Paris, we will not go to Paris." She wanted to ask J Burden to go along on the cruise, but Adele thought this was going too far, and the idea was dropped. The unhappy Beach followed his beloved across the Atlantic and joined her Uncle William K. aboard his yacht *The Valiant,* also in the Mediterranean, but the paths of the two vessels did not cross, probably by Emily's planning. By the end of the cruise enough detrimental anecdote on the subject of Beach had been imparted to Adele to induce her to give him up. In Paris, in the spring of 1894, she wrote:

Paris has never seemed less beautiful and less lovely than it does to me this year. There is a cold, cruel wickedness in it all. I feel chilled and depressed. The first news I heard when I arrived here two days ago was that Mr. Beach was in Paris. I never dreamed he was here. He wrote me he was going home the first of April. Would to God he had! They have told me things about him which made me cry myself to sleep the first night, and have made my heart and head ache since. He is leading openly a bad life here in Paris. . . . I remember so well Mr. Beach telling me once that if he lost me, all the good would go out of his life, and he would not care what became of him. I told him how cowardly I thought that was, and how miserably weak. But it is just what he has done.

There was one further encounter. "I saw him for the first time two days ago. He was walking with Mr. Cushing and another man, and I was driving with Papa. I don't think I bowed; I have a vague recollection of only looking and then of feeling horribly cold; then Papa said something, and two minutes later we were at the hotel. I was trembling all over and felt sick and dizzy."

And then it was over. Her not very wild oats had been sown, and she was ready for the hero of the tale. Creighton Webb was nasty enough to tell her that she had ruined his and Fred Beach's lives, and now was she going to ruin J Burden's? But indeed she had no such plans. In June she was able to write: "I do not feel like going to bed, and I do not feel like writing, and thinking makes me excited and nervous, and reading is out of the question. Of all, writing is the easiest, and it may have a quieting effect on my nerves. Somehow or other I don't quite understand or remember that J has told me that he likes me and that I have said 'yes' to him, and that he has held me in his arms and kissed me, and that I have kissed him often."

Her happiness was able to survive the opulent glow of jewels with which Vanderbilts and Burdens celebrated the engagement.

My wedding presents are beginning to come in faster and faster, over thirty now. The ones from Papa and Mamma and Uncle Corneil and Aunt Alice have completely taken away my breath. Papa gave me a gorgeous diamond sun, the largest one I have ever seen. Mother gave me a diamond and sapphire necklace, one that she has worn a little while herself and therefore all the dearer to me, and from Uncle Corneil a most gorgeous stomacher of diamonds and one enormous pearl. They sent it to me last Sunday evening, and I was so excited about it that I made J take me up in a hansom to the house so that I could thank them myself. Then we went up to J's house to show it to his father and mother. And he got me there his present for me and showed it to me first in the hansom by the glare of a street lamp. It is the loveliest diamond necklace, set in the most beautiful way. I can wear it as a collar, a tiara, or a pin. It is too dear of him to have given it to me; that and my engagement ring in one year are certainly enough to turn my head and quite spoil me.

The marriage was far happier than Gertrude's and Harry's. There were three children; there was travel and hunting and many parties and friends and charitable work. Like all Vanderbilts they built large houses, but they lived in them with grace. If J spent more time in Troy than Adele regarded as necessary, looking after a losing family business the income of which they did not need, at least he did not insist that she live there, nor did he begrudge her spending her own money for an additional house in Paris. They worked out their differences of taste and opinion amicably. Adele had a quality rare among the rich: that of always being able to enjoy what her money could buy. And enjoying it, she was able to make others enjoy it.

J died in 1932, and five years later Adele, at sixty-three, married

Richard Tobin, a bachelor even older, president of the Hibernia Bank in San Francisco and a former United States minister to the Netherlands. But he was perhaps the more congenial of her two spouses, being a musician, an amateur of the arts, and a favorite in international circles. Adele at the time was keeping another diary, since destroyed, but which she allowed me to read. The story of her second engagement had all the charm and innocence of what she had written in the nineties. There was even a reference to "Dick's outrageous behavior" in a taxi coming home from the theatre. But it was all right. They were almost engaged!

Widowed again, Adele died at eighty-seven in 1960. She left instructions that she was to be buried in the Burden Mausoleum in Troy.

CONSUELO

Consuelo, Duchess of Marlborough.

SOMETIME AROUND 1950, when Consuelo Vanderbilt Balsan was preparing to write her memoirs, to be entitled *The Glitter and the Gold,* she asked my advice as to form. I suggested that she open her book with a chapter on a picturesque and opulent American childhood in the eighteen-eighties and nineties, with sylvan scenes in Newport and a Prendergast picture of Central Park and its baby carriages and starchily uniformed nurses; then move swiftly on to dancing classes and balls in gilded ballrooms, and at last—bang—hit her reader with a chapter called "The High Price of Dukes." This would tell, in blunt terms, mixed with turgid legal euphuisms, the story of how her mother bought a peer and smashed her child's resistance. The idea would be to give the reader some of the same shock felt by the seventeen-year-old Consuelo when faced with the bargain that would make her, unloved and unloving, duchess of Marlborough.

She didn't like the idea at all. When I pointed out that there had been many books about American heiresses marrying European nobles, but that hers would be the most dramatic of all, involving as it would the greatest heiress and the greatest duke, she protested that, as her title would imply, Blenheim Palace was just the glitter and her real life, the one devoted to social work and to her second husband, Jacques Balsan, the gold. Well, that of course was her prerogative, and it would have been ungracious of me to insist that Blenheim Palace was what the public really wanted to read about.

"And of course I can't put in a book what a beast Marlborough was," she added pensively.

She did, however, allow her reader to deduce it. For this charming and beautiful old lady, though possessed of the greatest generosity of heart and mind, had been too cruelly treated by her mother and first husband ever to be able to forget it, even though she certainly forgave. In the end, half of her book would be devoted to the eleven years of her unhappy marriage to the duke. And so brilliant was her recorded success in England, so numerous her friendships among the political leaders of the day, and so dispassionate her account of how she was "bought" that some readers have surmised that she might not have been so badly treated, after all, that her mother, however bossy, may have known what was best for her, and that the duke, who had had also to give up love for a dowry indispensable to his impoverished estate, mightn't have been such a bad fellow—as dukes went.

I wonder if Consuelo would have minded this. She was always anxious to do justice to her mother, and at the very end of her life she was still talking of writing a second book on the great personalities she had known, of whom Alva would have been one. It was never her intention to settle old scores in *The Glitter and the Gold,* but rather to show how a woman could recover from an unfortunate first marriage in an uncongenial society and achieve a happy second union and a useful career in social work. And she does so. But I impenitently believe that her story would have been better told my way. It might have had some of the force and vigor of a Fielding novel, where the good characters are constantly threatened by the bad. And where the bad are really brutes.

If we put together the facts of Consuelo's coercion, as gleaned from her restrained narrative, separated from other episodes and descriptive passages, they are formidable enough. As a child, doing her lessons, she was obliged to wear a steel rod which ran down her spine and was strapped at her waist and over her shoulders. Another strap went around her forehead to the rod. It was almost impossible for her to write in so uncomfortable a position, but a good posture was obtained. On the beach she was allowed to bob up and down in the waves (she was never taught to swim) fully covered by a dark alpaca dress with drawers, long stockings, and a large hat to protect her from the sun. Picnics were abandoned as they involved flirtations, and she was not destined for any American male. Corporal punishment with a riding crop was freely administered by Alva herself. Yet so complete was the maternal domination of mind as well as body that when the door of the safe containing the family jewels failed to open one night when Consuelo's mother was dressing for dinner and it looked as if the great

Alva might have to sally forth unadorned, Consuelo rushed to her room and prayed fervently to God to avert such a catastrophe. The door opened at last; the Deity was on the side of parures. All her life Consuelo would sleep with a *veilleuse*; if so many bad things occurred in the daytime, who knew what might happen in the dark?

At seventeen she was introduced to the duke of Marlborough in London. "He seemed to me very young, although six years my senior, and I thought him good-looking and intelligent. He had a small aristocratic face with a large nose and rather prominent blue eyes. His hands, which he used in a fastidious manner, were well-shaped and he seemed inordinately proud of them." She went to Blenheim, but was not further impressed either with its glory or its master, and came away resolved not to marry him. Besides, she had a beau of her own now, an American, Winthrop Rutherfurd, handsome, rich, and good-natured, totally eligible in the eyes of every mother but the coronet-obsessed Alva. Consuelo somehow found the courage to tell her mother she was engaged.

The war now began in earnest. "On reaching Newport my life became that of a prisoner, with my mother and my governess (Miss Harper) as wardens. I was never out of their sight. Friends called but were told I was not at home. Locked behind those high walls—the porter had orders not to let me out unaccompanied—I had no chance of getting any word to my fiancé. I was helpless under my mother's total domination."

Yet even so, she managed to have one short dance with Rutherfurd, quickly interrupted, and to assure herself that he still cared. Alva now behaved like the maniac she may temporarily have become. She assured Consuelo that Rutherfurd was a philanderer, in love with a married woman and only interested in her money. She claimed he was sterile and that there was madness in his family. She finally went so far as to threaten that she would shoot him; Consuelo would be responsible for her mother's being hanged. When all else failed, she took to her bed, and her friend, Mrs. Jay, who was staying in the house, warned Consuelo that a fatal stroke would be the result of her callous indifference to the maternal feelings. I wonder if a little demon in purgatory is not giving Mrs. Jay an extra poke with his pitchfork for her officiousness. Consuelo, broken at last, authorized her to tell Ruthurfurd that she would not marry him.

Then Miss Harper, with the servility and reverence for rank of an English governess, went to work to expound on the opportunities for "usefulness and social service" that Consuelo would have as a duchess, until it began to seem to the poor girl that it was her duty not only to save her mother's life but to "live for others." Marlborough was summoned by the exultant Alva, and in early November they were wed.

It seems almost incredible. Could Rutherfurd not have gone to Consuelo's father? But we have seen in an earlier chapter that William K., separated from his virago of a wife and his children, was not a man to make a scene. Could Consuelo not have insisted on a longer delay? The answer seems to be that she was brainwashed. It is only surprising, I suppose, in view of the strength of character she was later to develop.

The picture we derive of the duke is of a petty, small-minded, snobbish, and rather cruel man who must have hated his wife because he had to marry her and because she was taller and richer and handsomer and infinitely more popular, even with his own set, than he. We see him on their wedding night, solemnly handing her cablegrams from the mighty of his homeland, including one from Queen Victoria, and looking to be sure that she was duly impressed. We see him in Paris choosing for her wardrobe not the prettiest but the most ostentatious dresses. We see him obliging her to study the peerage. We see *her* seeing him hide a china box to find out if the servants will notice its disappearance and enjoying the accusations of theft that ensue. He is a twin of Gilbert Osmond, Henry James's frigid dilettante in *The Portrait of a Lady*. How it must have galled him that his wife came to be considered the most beautiful thing in his beloved Blenheim!

Certainly she did the job well. Miss Harper's dim soul must have been bursting with pride. One can almost understand how Consuelo's old friend, Lord Curzon, could ask her, after she had become Madame Balsan, if it had been worth the "sacrifice."

"Sacrifice?" she inquired.

"Yes—to give up being the beautiful duchess of Marlborough, and all it meant."

And of course it had meant something, in the splendid sunset of British imperialism, to stand on the steps of the greatest of English country houses to greet the arriving prince and princess of Wales and their colorful escort. But Consuelo's head was never turned by what she saw as a snobbish and hierarchical society where the arrogance of the castle was equaled only by the unctuous servility of the cottages. She could play their game, however, when she had to, as when she blocked her husband's aunt in a crude attempt to usurp the authority of the mistress of Blenheim.

At one of my first dinner parties, to my surprise I found the ladies rising at a signal given by my husband's aunt, who was sitting next to him. Immediately aware of a concerted plan to establish her dominance, and warned by my neighbor Lord Chesterfield's exclamation, "Never have I seen anything so rude; don't move!" I nonetheless went to the door and meeting her, inquired in dulcet tones, "Are you ill, S?" "Ill?" she shrilled. "No, certainly not, why should I be ill?" "There surely was no other excuse for your hasty exit," I said calmly. She had the grace to blush; the other women hid their smiles, and never again was I thus challenged!

She had some of Alva's spirit, after all. It could not have been easy for her, still under twenty, in a strange land, surrounded by a large supercilious family-in-law, with a husband probably smirking at his aunt's little project, to take that stand. Fortunately Lord Chesterfield was a herald of the wide support that was coming her way. Only her use of the initial "S" to conceal the aunt's identity was disingenuous. It had been clearly revealed on an earlier page as Lady Sarah Churchill Wilson.

Consuelo had been cut off from her father's family by her parents' divorce, but after her marriage she was free to see them again, and the Vanderbilt cousins flocked to Blenheim to view her in her glory. Her favorite was Adele Sloane Burden, who related to me in a later year how Consuelo's name had become a password in English society.

At a large house party Adele had found herself at the same bridge table with Margot Asquith.

"Who are you?" the wife of the future prime minister abruptly demanded.

Adele explained that she was Mrs. James Burden, from New York.

"Yes, but who *are* you?" Margot repeated, with the rough insistence of her class and era.

Adele again quietly identified herself.

Margot shrugged and went on with the game, but later in the evening, when she had had a chance to talk to someone better informed, she came back to prove the correctness of her initial assumption.

"I *knew* you were somebody. You're Consuelo's cousin!"

Perhaps because Alva's three children had the good fortune to inherit her brains and not her vile temper, they were the most successful of William Henry's grandchildren. Yet so strong is the hangover of the Puritan ethic, though now transferred to the marketplace, that I have read descriptions, in books and articles about the Vanderbilts, of Consuelo's younger brothers, William K., Jr., and Harold Vanderbilt, as frivolous types who devoted their lives to sport and games. But to untold thousands of Americans the father of contract bridge might be deemed a father of *their* country. And if card players owe such a debt to Harold, the lovers of marine animals must owe a comparable one to William K., Jr., who roamed the Pacific in his yachts *Ara* and *Alva* to capture for his marine museum on Long Island such rare specimens of fish with such wonderful Edward Lear or Lewis Carroll names as the golden flutemouth, the calico razor wrasse, the Moorish idol, the fringed pipefish, and the blueline butterfly. Unless it be frivolous not to be engaged in the making of money, such accomplishments should not be so branded.

Harold Vanderbilt gave to the ancient game of whist a worldwide popularity by converting it to the principle of the French Plafond. Games now had to be bid if they were to be scored, and bonuses were given for slams. Two years later, in 1927, the Whist Club formally drew up and adopted his rules, and the Portland Club of London consulted him in establishing the Contract Code. Harold wrote two texts on the subject: *Contract Bridge* (1929) and *New Contract Bridge* (1930). Some may find it distasteful to contemplate the enormous role that this game plays on social occasions and in the lives of the elderly, retired, and ill, or that it formerly played in the long days of middle- and upper-income women before work became the prerogative of both sexes, but I could argue that Harold, for better or worse, was a major force in American social history.

Certainly nobody would wish to deprive him of credit for his contribution to the noble sport of racing sailboats. In 1930 he formed the syndicate that built the *Enterprise* to defend the America's Cup against the challenge of Sir Thomas Lipton's *Shamrock V.* Harold supervised the construction of the vessel, experimenting with a higher, narrower rig and a duraluminian mast, and was skipper in the first four races in which it defeated its rival. Both in cards and in boats he was a brilliant engineer.

GRACE

The twin Vanderbilt brownstones on Fifth Avenue between
Fifty-first and Fifty-second streets. No. 640 on the left was the
residence of William Henry and was "modernized" by Grace.

GRACE WILSON, who in 1896 married Cornelius Vanderbilt III, "Neily," son of Cornelius II and Alice, is certainly the best known of all the Mrs. Vanderbilts and possibly the best known of all the family after the commodore himself. From her marriage to her death in 1953, almost sixty years later, she was a regular feature in society columns and came to be considered by journalists as the undisputed successor to Mrs. Astor as queen of Gotham. And certainly the journalists should know, as both the title and the position were their inventions.

Grace differed from Alva, her husband's onetime aunt by marriage, in that she possessed a lively imagination, or at least as much of that quality as was needed to be able to foresee not only what it would be like to be a society leader, but that it would be a role that would never—not even for a day or night—lose for her the least portion of its charm. Grace owed her curious importance in the newspaper version of American social history to the fact that she saw herself exactly as the reporters chose to describe her. She was at all times, to herself and to them, a "queen," a "dowager" (a term not necessarily associated with widowhood), a "chatelaine," a "grande dame." Her parties were "exclusive" and her guest list "impeccable." In her last years, arriving at the opera, leaving the opera, surrounded by flash bulbs, her hair swathed in her famous "headache band," holding up her purse before her face in a feint of reluctance to be photographed, she and her accompanying chorus of reporters played out to the end the little ballet of which neither seemed to tire.

The Wilsons, like Alva's family, the Smiths, were from the South, but they had been enriched rather than impoverished by the war.

115

Cornelius Vanderbilt IV, in his life of his mother, *Queen of the Golden Age,* denies that his maternal grandfather, Richard Wilson, was a war profiteer, but admits that the reputation clung to him. At any rate, the Wilsons were probably more socially comfortable in New York than in their native Georgia. Not only was Yankeeland full of men who had also made a good thing out of the conflict, but the victims of the Wilsons, if victims there had been, were the defeated and now powerless enemy. Certainly the Wilson reputation did not prevent Grace's older siblings from making the most brilliant matches of their day. Mary became Mrs. Ogden Goelet; Belle's husband, the Honorable Michael Herbert, was first secretary of the British legation in Washington; and Orme married the Caroline Astor whose threatened quadrille had brought about her mother's capitulation to the Vanderbilts.

Did any lingering memory of shoddy equipment supplied to beleaguered Confederate soldiers sharpen the ambition of Grace and her sisters to put all that behind them in the sheer dazzle of their new alliances? One doubts it. They were fine, handsome women who took naturally to a high stage of life, and Grace, the youngest and prettiest, may naturally have dreamed of surpassing them all. And how better could she do that than becoming Mrs. Cornelius Vanderbilt III and, in the due course of events, "Mrs. Vanderbilt"?

Grace was very much an ornament of the New York and Newport social scenes, with brilliant excursions to those of London and Paris, and everyone assumed that her obvious (too obvious?) goal of a great match would be easily attained. But why did it go on so long? She was twenty-five. Or twenty-six? Even older, some whispered. By the time young Neily (younger than she indeed) fell in love with her, and her dream of dreams seemed about to be realized, the young couple faced a roadblock. Neily's parents flatly refused to accept her as a daughter-in-law.

Why? Nobody knows for sure. They might have considered her, that deeply serious and devout couple, too flighty and worldly for their boy, too given up to dinners and dances, but this would have been true of half the young crowd that came to The Breakers or Fifty-eighth Street. Was she—a graver fault—a flirt? Or even worse? Did Henry James, who knew many Vanderbilts, have something like this in mind when he created his character, Julia Bride, who might have been so much less lovely to the "quiet, cultured, earnest" heir to "enormous wealth and crushing respectability" had she been only "well, a little prepared to answer questions"?

The older Vanderbilts certainly had a reason, imagined or not, for their unremitting hostility, for they were not people of hasty or ill-informed judgments, and they were devoted to their children. Cornelius II not only refused to receive Grace; he changed his will when the young couple married without his sanction, giving Neily's heir-apparent share to his younger brother, Alfred, and cutting Neily off with a scant million. And this was the will that was probated, only three years later, when Cornelius II died, still unreconciled to his oldest son. Alice would come around to accepting Grace, but not for several more years.

The only proffered explanation that would seem to fit so fierce an opposition is that Grace had been somehow involved with Neily's older brother, the handsome and adored William, who had died of typhoid at the age of twenty, while still a student at Yale. Grace might well have likened herself to Princess Mary of Teck, who, deprived of the heir to the British throne by the same disease, had docilely performed her dynastic duty by transferring her mild affections to his younger brother, George. But Cornelius II may have seen it in a very different light. He may have seen Grace as a gold digger determined to have a Vanderbilt and not too particular as to which.

Neily had stuck to his guns. He had asked this beautiful young woman to marry him, and that was that. If the inheritance had to go, so be it. Grace must have had some nervous apprehension about the future when her husband's parents boycotted her wedding, but she had every reason to suppose they would relent in the end. Parents usually did, particularly after the arrival of the first baby. She could not have foreseen the early death of Neily's implacable father or the horrid publicity of their disinheritance. Fortunately Alfred gave Neily six million from his lion's share which, added to Grace's own fortune, allowed her to embark on her long career of entertaining. And on George Vanderbilt's death in 1914, No. 640 Fifth Avenue, the great brownstone cube that the Herter brothers had erected for William Henry, passed under the latter's will to Neily, and Grace was able to remodel it and make it the social center of the avenue.

She never drew any distinction between income and principal. She spent what she had or could get her hands on and spent it lavishly. In the later years much of the capital was gone, 640 had been sold, and the upkeep of Neily's yacht had been undertaken by his sisters, but the great banquets went on to the end.

Neily's life, in the long aftermath of his tempestuous romance, was pathetically anticlimactic. He was a sober, serious man with a fine mind for engineering and locomotive design—one of his inventions was even of importance to the New York Central—and he became a brigadier general and served in France in the First World War. But something went wrong. It might have been simply the bitter disillusionment of finding that the woman for whom he had given up the position of chief of the clan cared only for the parties in which she frittered away his settlement. He seems to have inherited his father's puritanical sense of duty about what was expected of a Vanderbilt, without the means to justify the presumption, or the imagination to turn it into something useful, or even the hedonism to enjoy it. More and more, as he grew older he lived apart from his wife and her parties, taking long cruises on his yacht, the *Winchester,* seeking solace in drink. His son, Cornelius IV, found him a stern and strict parent who deeply disapproved of his chosen career of journalism. Was there an aspect of subconscious jealousy that the son should have the freedom the father had missed?

Grace could never understand what ailed him. She had what *she* wanted. Why could he not see what fun it was? She was one of those who can find perfect satisfaction in the constant decoration and adornment of life, concentrating largely on meals, dress, and rooms. There was a way, there *had* to be a way, and just the right way, too, of arranging one's externals, from the breakfast tray carried to one's bedside in the morning to the setting of a dinner table for forty at night, with eight courses all served in an hour. No detail was too small to be overlooked by a careful housekeeper and hostess, and the guests, fitted into the setting of French furniture and tapestries, had to be chosen with the same care as the chairs on which they sat: for their clothes, their manners, their pedigrees and, best of all, their titles—if they had them.

Cornelius IV describes how his mother organized even a simple family picnic:

When we went on a family picnic, there was no such nonsense as sitting on the ground and using paper plates and napkins. Instead, a carriage went ahead to the picnic site with two footmen, a maid, and one or two grooms. These servants set up a table under the trees with a white linen cloth and some of our best silverware and crystal. When we arrived on horseback, everything would be ready. The food was carried in English wicker baskets and consisted of cold consommé, in thermos bottles, and ham or chicken sandwiches on bread which was sliced very, very thin. Tomato and lettuce salad with olive oil and vinegar dressing, French rolls, many kinds of delicious flaky French pastry prepared by our chef, and apples, pears, nectarines and peaches. Often we had clotted cream spread on bread and topped with homemade strawberry jam.

What about friends, family, love? But Grace had all those things, didn't she? A beautifully dressed little daughter, a son in velvet knickers, an admired and distinguished husband? And friends? Had any house in America more people passing through it? To Grace what the fashionable portraitist painted, what the polite guest uttered in leaving, what the society reporter reported, was simply truth.

She probably never knew how she embarrassed her family. In the years following the First World War she arranged a proud display in a prominent vitrine in her parlor at No. 640. The guest who examined it saw an ordinary army canteen, a tin plate, and a knife, fork, and spoon. A card informed him that these utensils were the very ones that his hostess's son had used as an army private in France. That a Vanderbilt should have been reduced to such humble equipment in the service of his country Grace considered an edifying spectacle for her callers. Did General Vanderbilt ever notice the exhibit? If he did, he probably simply shuddered and looked the other way. He knew remonstrance was hopeless.

Cornelius IV asked his parents once why they didn't get a divorce.

"People in our position don't get divorces," was his father's stiff reply.

His mother's was more passionate. "But I love your father!" she cried. And in her way no doubt she did.

"In her last years," her son records,

her eyesight began to fail. She had only spots of clear vision, as if she were looking through the wrong end of a telescope. Her oculist felt that her condition could be much improved by glasses, but although Mother was constantly ordering new pairs, she was much too vain to wear them. Now as she sat upon a red velvet settee in a gold lamé gown, a golden bandeau about her snow-white head, greeting the hundreds of friends who always came to her glittering receptions, she could only recognize those who came within her very narrow range of vision.

"Who is it, darling? Who is coming now?" she would inquire brightly, clinging to my hand.

I never liked the duke of Windsor so well as the night he sat next to Mother at dinner and carefully, with an air of tender solicitude, cut into small morsels the slice of roast beef she could only dimly perceive in front of her.

It seems the right moment to take leave of her.

JOHN SINGER SARGENT

Florence V. Twombly by John Singer Sargent.

SARGENT, in common with Holbein and Van Dyck, was an international painter of portraits who did his major work in England. It was in his studio in London's Tite Street, during the eighteen-eighties and nineties, and in this century up to 1907, when he gave up painting what he derisively called "paughtraits," that he re-created on canvas the world of the Anglo-American upper classes. His success was as great as that of his two mentioned predecessors, but his posthumous reputation has had a bumpier time.

That it should have taken a nosedive right after his death in 1925 is surely attributable, at least in part, to the distastefulness of his subject matter to liberal minds. What could have seemed more trivial, more archaic, more socially irresponsible, even more vicious, in the grim years of depression and world war, than those strutting peers and peeresses, those lavishly dressed Yankee millionairesses, those belaced and beribboned children, those yapping lap dogs, those gleaming parlors and stately parks? Roger Fry summed up the attitude of the opposition: "That Sargent was taken for an artist will perhaps seem incredible to the rising generation."

The portrait painters of the more distant past have an easier time with critics. The court of Henry VIII, which lives today so vividly in the art of Holbein, awing us with the pale, set intensity of those faces confronting the remorseless game of politics and death, a game that Tudor statesmen seemed fated to play even when they faced hopeless odds, arouses no resentment in us. It is too far away, and, anyway, didn't the bad guys get their comeuppance in the end? Didn't even the wicked old cuckolded king die in agony? And who could hold a grudge against the beautiful, doomed cavaliers of the Caroline court or the sad, pensive, charming monarch who lost his foolish head? Yet I daresay a Roundhead art critic could have been as devastating about Van Dyck as Fry was about Sargent.

We are now far enough away from Sargent's era to have lost much of our indignation over its shortcomings. We can admit that his "Lord Ribblesdale" rivals Van Dyck's "Charles I," that it is the perfect portrait of a British aristocrat of the time. The tall, gaunt, graceful figure, whose height is emphasized by the silhouette, stands before us in the hunting habit of the master of Buckhounds, holding a whip that he will hardly have to apply but that he would easily be capable of using. The expression on the long, handsome face is gravely courteous; there is even a hint of humor in the serenely gazing eyes; the man is obviously intelligent and of strong character. But part of his strength comes from his absolute acceptance of his social position and his faith in the hierarchy in which he is the fourth Baron Ribblesdale, one of the richest of the peers. And the fact that, despite features worthy of a prime minister, he chooses to be represented as a master of Buckhounds has its own message about the role that the peerage still played in 1902.

There probably has never been an artist who had an easier start than Sargent. His early years and education joined perfectly with his talent to create a painter suited precisely to the world he was to paint. His parents were American expatriates who lived a migratory life in rented villas and apartments in old palazzi, from Rome to Dresden, following the warm weather north, except when cheaper prices pointed in a chillier direction. They saw other expatriates, the local gentry, and an occasional artist, but they had little to do with the makers and doers of the business and political worlds. They were tireless sight-seers and sketchers, and young John grew up in an atmosphere where beautiful things and the reproduction of them were deemed of the first importance.

Sargent had very little formal schooling; tutors and voluminous reading, in addition to the parental sight-seeing, constituted the bulk of his education. He had no training in science or law or economics, and all his life he was quite helpless in practical matters, leaving the large sums of money that he ultimately earned to be invested by others. But what saved him from the dilettantism that may have to some extent informed the family circle was the all-seeing painter's eye that he was given every opportunity and encouragement to develop. His father had wanted him to go into the U.S. Navy, but as this prospect had little charm to a youth already intent on landscapes and human faces and who did not visit his native land until his twentieth year, in the mid-1870s, the indulgent parent did not press the matter. When his family moved to Paris, John was sent to study under Carolus-Duran, the most popular teacher of the day, who encouraged his pupil's taste both for what was best in the old academic art and for what was needed to refresh it from the new and exciting school of Impressionism.

Thus, unlike most young artists, Sargent was able to follow his natural bent and to begin at an early age re-creating the world that it had been his passion to observe. It is not surprising that he rapidly attained technical mastery, and Henry James wrote in an article about his work: "In an altogether exceptional degree does he give us the sense that the intention and the art of carrying it out are for him one and the same thing. . . . perception with him is already by itself a kind of execution. . . . It is as if painting were pure tact of vision, a simple manner of feeling."

James concluded that Sargent's "Lady with the Rose" and his portrait of the Boit children offer the "slightly uncanny spectacle of a talent which on the very threshold of its career has nothing more to learn." This sentence aptly hits the essence of Sargent's genius and its greatest problem.

It sometimes seems that Sargent brought nothing but his eyes to his art. He never went in for theories of painting, and he was inclined to be impatient with art critics. The only important things to him were looking and painting, not talking or writing. He had no particular interest in politics, domestic or international, or in ideologies or philosophies. He was concerned with the immediate thing that he could see or hear or touch. Besides painting, he loved to read fiction and poetry, in German, French, and Italian as well as English, and he played the piano with the skill of one who might have been a concert pianist had he elected that field. But his indifference to larger human issues (as opposed to private relationships, where he was always warm and responsive) was sometimes distressing to his friends. Henry James, for example, who had passionately espoused the Allied cause in the Great War and who had become a British subject to express his impatience at the failure of America to come in, could not understand

Sargent's detachment. But how unreal the conflict was to the painter was shown by his remark on a visit to the front as late as 1918: "I suppose there is no fighting on Sundays."

Hostile critics have jumped on this aspect of Sargent's nature to discount the intellectual and emotional content of his work. Roger Fry wrote of "The Wyndam Sisters": "Since Sir Thomas Lawrence's time no one has been able thus to seize the exact cachet of fashionable life, or to render it in paint with a smartness and piquancy which so exactly corresponds to the social atmosphere itself. Sargent appears to harbor no imaginations that he could not easily avow at the afternoon tea-table he so brilliantly depicts."

Sargent himself gave some support to this kind of criticism by his answer to Joseph Pulitzer's suggestion that he explore his sitter's character in conversation before starting on the likeness: "No, I paint what I see. Sometimes it makes a good portrait; so much the better for the sitter. Sometimes it does not; so much the worse for the both of us. But I don't dig beneath the surface for things that don't appear before my eyes."

But does it really matter that Sargent had no imaginations that he could not "easily avow at the afternoon tea-table"? What he was intent on bringing out was as much of a personality as a disciplined social figure would allow to appear on the surface—or would not be able to prevent appearing on the surface. Deeply indoctrinated in the mannerisms, the stances, the poses, the clothes, the background furniture, the makeup, the hairdos, the smiles, and the reservations of people in society, he was able to probe as deeply as a portraitist need. At least so I claim for the moment. He did not have to talk at length to Asher Wertheimer to catch the craftiness and worldliness, the perfect taste coupled with the graspingness of the fine arts dealer.

Consider what we see in his portrait of Madame Edouard Pailleron, an early work. The wife of the popular playwright stands on a lawn, ruffled by a faint breeze, although she is dressed formally in black. It is as if she had been asked to come out of the house for a moment to pose for a photograph. The way she holds her skirt and almost frowns might indicate a faint impatience at being kept from her duties as a hostess within. Indeed, she seems to belong more to the marble balustrade in the background than to the lawn and the leaves. And yet one receives no sense of an artificial being. If Madame Pailleron is an elegant hostess, she is also a highly competent household manager. It is easy to imagine her in rougher garb, weeding and hoeing. She is unmistakably Gallic.

The first Mrs. Henry White (Margaret Ruthurfurd), on the other hand, is, equally unmistakably, American. She stands, tall, proud, and beautiful, with the confidence wrought of grace, discipline, lineage, and money, and yet for all this she is not quite sure that she is going to be, in the glare of London "crushes," quite the success she deserves to be. But she may be if she tries, and God knows she will try! One can feel it in the tense resolution of her stare and in the way the fingers of her left hand grip her opera glasses. Allan Nevins, Henry White's biographer, told me once of a contemporary of his subject who had described the difference between Mrs. White's greeting of a duke and a commoner as "awe-inspiring."

A second American woman, Lady Astor, does not have Mrs. White's intensity; she is radiantly confident of the inexhaustible supply of her own beauty and energy. In this charming picture Sargent evokes all the fervor and idealism of a New World turning back to conquer the Old. It is almost too much. Do we catch a hint of the bossy, eccentric old parliamentarian-to-be in the foxy smile, the almost-too-coy pose of this lovely young woman? Perhaps I am going too far, but if Sargent saw all in a face, he may have seen the future as well.

When the sitter had no distinct character of feature, Sargent made up for it as best he could in the dress and setting. Mrs. Hugh Hammersley is a case in point. One sees that she was a vapid, amiable, very pretty Englishwoman, but the dignity of her rich pink dress and of the lavish gold background redeems the picture. Henry Adams was fascinated by this portrait. Was Sargent intentionally insulting the whole money culture? he wondered hopefully. Was he trying to expose the soul (assuming there were one) of the female "goldbug"? I suppose Sargent would have replied that he was painting what he saw. But what did he *see*?

Even when a sitter was not personally sympathetic to him, even when she posed reluctantly and then refused to finish, as did the lazy, shallow Madame Pierre Gautreau, he was able to make a masterpiece. She stands before us as "Madame X," the embodiment of female vanity, with nothing, absolutely nothing to justify it but the incomparable beauty of her body and skin, which she shows off in a pose so effectively dramatic as to excuse its absurdity.

Sargent was to some extent the victim of his own success. The world thronged to his studio, and no matter what he charged for a portrait, it was willing to pay. Friends intervened to plead with him to take this or that sitter; it was hard to say no. A popular cartoon showed him looking from his studio window in despair at the long line of elegant carriages clogging Tite Street. Eventually the sheer quantity of the work began to take its toll on the quality. One feels that the artist is bored.

This ennui can be seen by contrasting "The Wyndham Sisters," of 1899, with "The Marlborough Family," done six years later. The former shows the master at the height of his powers; the dazzling white of the dresses against the somber background makes it a dramatic triumph. The duke and duchess, on the other hand, standing in a stiff, unlikely pose with two sons and two Blenheim spaniels on a grand marble stairway under the draped war banners of the first duke, seem merely pompous. Consuelo's beauty, it is true, almost redeems the picture; one is tempted to call it "The Apotheosis of the Vanderbilts." They have crossed the Atlantic and bought Blenheim Palace. It seems fitting that the heiress stands a head higher than her husband.

And had they bought Sargent, too? Is that where I come out? He indeed painted four generations of the family, including William Henry's widow, two of her sons, two daughters, and several of her grandchildren and great-grandchildren. It makes up a gallery that seems to echo Adams's question of what the devil Sargent was up to. Contemplating the indubitably flattered Florence Vanderbilt Twombly, regal in gold, or the equally flattered Margaret Vanderbilt Shepard, imperial in scarlet, I do begin to suspect that more than a few drops of the seemingly inescapable vulgarity of that opulent era have found their insidious way into the very heart of the master's art. One can see why Sargent, his pockets crammed with gold, sought to give up the "paughtrait" business in 1907.

It remained, one is happy to add, for him to do his finest watercolors, and charcoal sketches, some as good as any of his portraits.

JAY GOULD

"Portrait in Brownstone":
Jay Gould's residence at 579 Fifth Avenue.

I REMEMBER a daughter of Winthrop Chanler, prominent sportsman and socialite of the early years of this century, telling me of a family breakfast in New York in 1910, or thereabouts, when she was describing to her father a debutante dinner party she had attended the night before. "Who'd you sit next to?" he growled from behind his newspaper. "Young Jay Gould." The paper fell. "You didn't speak to him, I hope?"

Such was the reputation in New York social circles of that young man's late grandfather, the man who managed to seize control of both the Union Pacific and Western Union and who died one of the richest and most hated men in the country, the archvillain of the Vanderbilt era. But there is always room for revisionist history. It used to be argued that there were two types of nineteenth-century robber barons: those who, like Commodore Vanderbilt, John D. Rockefeller, and J. P. Morgan, were more creative than destructive, who in the long run made some significant contribution to the industrialization of America, and those who, like Jay Gould, Jim Fisk, and Daniel Drew, simply preyed on weak businesses, slipping slyly into control, watering their stock, looting their treasuries, and passing the inflated carcasses on to a gullible public in return for the latter's hard-earned savings. Some revisionists would go so far as to lump the two categories together, endowing both with Theodore Roosevelt's label: "malefactors of great wealth."

The commodore himself detested Gould, and even insulted his looks: "No one can have such a countenance as his and still be honest!" But then the commodore was large and handsome, and Gould, small, puny-limbed, and hollow-chested. And he had had the temerity to lick Vanderbilt in several rounds of the battle for Erie. I suspect an inclination, on the part of some of the commodore's supporters, as exemplified by that archpriest of the New York Central, Depew, to identify the louder and more physically vigorous of the business leaders with earlier pioneers, associating them with the frontier and stockades and killing Indians, and to contrast them unfavorably with such etiolated urban types as they imagined Gould to be, creeping out of the cellars to gnaw on the corpses of stricken corporations.

But any type can be romanticized. Byron made a hero out of his ruthless corsair. Maury Klein, a recent apologist for Gould, portrays him thus:

At forty-three Gould had already fought the wars of Wall Street for nearly two decades, and his body had begun its retreat toward the hollow shell it would soon become. There seemed barely enough flesh to cover even his frail frame. His thinning black hair had receded to expose a high, cerebral forehead and make his large ears even more prominent. The wiry thicket that masked his lower face contrasted with his complexion, swarthy yet tinged with the pallor of one who seldom saw sunlight. There was about his appearance a quality of abstraction, of intellectuality, as if brain had sucked body dry to fuel its own incessant needs. Even his eyes, those dark pools of mystery, confirmed this impression, whether glowing softly or fixed with laserlike intensity or glazed with preoccupation, as if his mind had gone to dwell on some remote place beyond the reach of ordinary mortals.

Certainly, by the standards of our more regulated economy, the business activities of both Vanderbilt and Gould were carried on in reckless disregard of the public. But distinctions can still be drawn between exploitations of the latter, if only in degree. Henry Adams, who could never be accused of partiality to the class he defined (as we shall explore in a later chapter) as "goldbugs," deemed Vanderbilt "one of the most respectable of the great operators," who at least acted in the interests of his corporations. Gould, on the other hand, according to Adams, cheated his companies and the public alike, making no distinction between right and wrong in matters of speculation:

"In this respect Gould was probably as honest as the mass of his fellows, according to the moral standard of the street; but he was an uncommonly fine and unscrupulous intriguer, skilled in the processes of stock gambling and passably indifferent to the praise or censure of society."

I think the last clause may give us a clue to Gould's extraordinary unpopularity. In an age where the Almighty was invoked at every congregation of rascals, where a virtuous label had to be solemnly attached to the most blatant acts of self-aggrandizement, where the commodore himself, as we have already seen, could be seriously described as "puffed with divine greed," it was intolerable that a man should become a multi-millionaire without offering the smallest lip service to the prevailing precepts of fatuity. Had Gould even boasted of his turpitude with the shameless bravado of his swashbuckling partner, Fisk, who had reassured his cohorts in a tight spot that nothing had been lost but honor, he might have been in part forgiven. But his silence doomed him.

His very lifestyle may have contributed to his reputation for deceit. Could one really credit the sincerity of this soft-spoken little man who shunned society and ballrooms, seeming to prefer the placid domesticity of his sober brownstone and the company of the simple wife to whom he was always faithful and the children whom he lovingly spoiled? Was there not something more appropriately Mephistophelian in the man who retreated on weekends to his strange Gothic castle on the Hudson to sniff the exotic flowers in his many greenhouses?

But the truth was less romantic. Gould's lifelong passion, from the schooldays of his simple farm upbringing in Delaware County, New York, where at the age of fourteen and to the delight of future biographers he wrote an essay entitled "Honesty Is the Best Policy," had been to get around or on top of the bigger guys. Born at a time when money was the trick to that game, he became a money juggler. In the Middle Ages, no doubt, he would have mastered theology and become a cardinal, though of the political rather than the priestly kind. He faced each new challenge with the zeal of a young computer expert of our own day who is delighted when his genius evolves a method of entering the systems of others and destroying with one pressed key thousands of stored memories.

Farming, needless to say, was not for him. He worked as a store clerk and a surveyor, promoted a mousetrap, built a plank road, and helped found a small bank. A partner in one of his early ventures, a leather business, committed suicide when he learned that Gould had misused his name and money. Gould moved to New York and married the daughter of a rich grocer. The Civil War was on, but he paid it scant attention. Its function to him, unless it brought a chance for a lucrative army contract, was simply to remove those competitors who were fool enough to enlist. He now became a member of Smith Martin & Company, stockbrokers who traded heavily in Erie Railroad stock, and his real career as an acquirer and destroyer began.

What he and his partners, Drew and Fisk, did to Erie may be the shabbiest chapter in railroad history. They used the company as their personal treasury, and its stock, issued at their will, as trumps in their card game of market maneuvers, until the line was in receivership and Gould, at least, was rich. No stake was too high for him. When he turned his attention to the fantastic scheme of cornering the gold market, he secured the cooperation of no less a person than the President of the United States, conning Ulysses S. Grant through his bribed brother-in-law into putting a stop to government sales of bullion while Gould was buying it. Grant, at last alerted to the national danger, ordered the sale of gold to burst Gould's bubble, but the latter, on notice as always of what was about to happen, pulled out of the market in the nick of time.

He put together, before his death in his middle fifties in 1892, one of the greatest fortunes of the time, almost a hundred million dollars. Yet he never showed, except for his greenhouses, much interest in spending it, and certainly little in giving it away. All that he cared about where money was concerned—and he was not concerned with very much else—was making it. But making it always had to be in a game worthy of his genius. I doubt that he would have stooped to pick up a gold piece on the street or even to smile at a rich relative (had he had one) to induce a legacy. No, *his* money had to be money obtained by his wits, at the expense of another, even at lethal cost, for only the crushing of a victim would reveal the true magnitude of the victory. Gould, as Matthew Josephson has said, "seemed to enjoy most the role of the one against all: self-contained, impassive to all pleas or reproaches, he seemed content with his loneliness."

Maury Klein, his defender, tries to see in Gould's ultimate taking over of the Union Pacific Railroad a change of heart and a resolve to be a more constructive businessman.

What drove Jay to undertake this task remains an intriguing mystery. It could not have been simply the desire for gain, for there were quicker, less taxing ways of making money. Perhaps the immensity of the challenge appealed to him. Possibly, too, his tarnished reputation had begun to bother him. Although he would never admit to such a concern, he may have seen in the Union Pacific a chance to erase the stigma attached to his name. Whatever his motives Jay identified himself with the road in a way that transcended his usual ability to weave corporate and self-interest inextricably together. A new phase in his career had opened. He did not leave the market or cease his speculative forays; nor did he confine his activities to the Union Pacific. But he had taken hold of the road, and he did not mean to let it go.

But was there any larger road to be exchanged for it? Klein has to admit that Gould may not have comprehended his own dreams. "Like other men driven by demons, he may well have become prisoner of his own momentum."

I agree that Gould may have been driven by a demon. But the saddest thing to me in his story is that that demon seems very much around today. I am afraid that Jay Gould would have felt quite comfortable on our Wall Street of 1989.

AUGUSTUS
SAINT-GAUDENS

THE ARTISTS of the American Renaissance, who attempted in the final years of the last century to re-create the brilliant flowering of *Cinquecento* Italy, were a fortunate lot. The frontier had been pushed into the Pacific and the great railroads built, and prosperous Americans of the new upper class were anxious to invest their new riches in new mansions and furnishings. Cornelius Vanderbilt II employed Saint-Gaudens, John La Farge, and Louis Tiffany to embellish the interior of his château on Fifth Avenue, and his brother George hung portraits of his architect, Hunt, and of his landscape designer, Olmsted, in Biltmore. To the enlightened of the period America had plenty of room for artists as well as businessmen, for Stanford White *and* J. P. Morgan, for John Singer Sargent *and* John D. Rockefeller, for William Dean Howells *and* E. H. Harriman.

Augustus Saint-Gaudens started life in circumstances humbler than those of other American Renaissance giants. His mother, an Irish beauty, and his father, a French shoemaker, emigrated to New York shortly after their son's birth in 1848. The senior Saint-Gaudens established a fashionable shoe shop in Manhattan. He apprenticed his son to a cameo cutter and encouraged his artistic interests, but he was not able to give him much financial assistance when the young man went to study in the École des Beaux-Arts in Paris. Success came early to Saint-Gaudens, however. In 1876 he won the commission for the bronze statue of Admiral David Farragut in Madison Square Park, and other commissions soon followed. He was able to slip easily enough into a glittering world in which he could lunch with Henry James at the Century Club one day and dine at the Players' with his frequent collaborator, Stanford White, the next. What is more, he shared, even

139

though less articulately, the cultural and political values held by these more sophisticated and more deeply educated men. He believed that America's governing classes were by and large leading it ably forward along the trail blazed by Washington and Lincoln (the latter being the subject of one of his most successful works).

Well, was this wrong? Do artists have to hate the rich and powerful? Must they always be hurling stones at the establishment? Perhaps not. But when they take on the stamp of their era as Saint-Gaudens did his, it is much remarked upon—usually with disapproval—by their immediate successors. It takes them some time to live it down. It is quite possible that Saint-Gaudens will cast a larger shadow in the next century than in ours. Perhaps that era will better understand a man who, however closely affiliated with the mood of the eighteen-eighties and nineties, still thought of himself as a *Cinquecento* artist.

Henry Adams, who traveled to Amiens with him to study the cathedral, made this observation: ". . . in mind and person Saint-Gaudens was a child of Benvenuto Cellini's, mothered in an American cradle." And so in a way he was. Like Cellini he was a consummate craftsman, and he introduced heroic realism to post–Civil War American sculpture. But his heroic sculpture was a very different thing from what Cellini and his contemporaries were trying to express. They would portray power and strength in a condottiere, for example, without in any way having to endorse—or condemn—the issues for which the man was fighting. The power and force of the subject were all the artist needed, even if they were used to burn towns and massacre innocent civilians. But Saint-Gaudens needed to admire the figures he sculpted, and he had little difficulty in doing so.

In 1897 he completed for the capitol in Boston the monument of Robert Gould Shaw leading his company of black soldiers, and in 1903 his equestrian statue of General Sherman for Grand Army Plaza in New York. Neither the angel hovering over Shaw nor the Victory leading Sherman were as artificial to Saint-Gaudens as they would have been to the cynical Cellini. I think he actually believed in some sort of divine inspiration. Even the hooded figure in Rock Creek Cemetery commemorating Henry Adams's wife, Clover, a suicide at forty-one, somehow manages, by suggesting the peace that passeth understanding, to place a discreet veil over the agnosticism of the Adamses. Saint-Gaudens made his concept of a beautiful world into a beautiful vision for us.

But we of course have lost these faiths and with them the ability to respond to Saint-Gaudens's art as so many of his contemporaries did. Instead, we look at it with questions born of hindsight and skepticism. Should the Civil War have been fought at all? Did God really care what Saint-Gaudens's Bishop Brooks was preaching to the Boston Brahmins? Didn't Lincoln look down a bit on blacks, and isn't there a hint of racial condescension in the sculpting of Shaw's soldiers? And as for the brooding figure in Rock Creek Cemetery, it may be beautiful, but can it make us forget Adams's anti-Semitism and snobbishness? The new type of puritan morality of our times has no patience with this amiable sculptor's sentimentalities.

Yet when I turn back to Saint-Gaudens's work, including the portrait bas-reliefs—those wonderful, grave, reflective men, women, and children, so subtly conceived and so exquisitely rendered—I have a sense that the American Renaissance may have been a better time in which to live than ours. Its people seem so serious, so high-minded. They seem so determined to make a better and more beautiful world, so concerned with order and dignity. I envy their apparent tranquillity. I wish I could share their sense of purpose and progress.

EDMUND C. STANTON

Edmund C. Stanton.

H E WAS my mother's uncle, a grave, tall, slender gentleman, always elegantly dressed (he sent his shirts to Paris to be cleaned), a minor ornament and to some extent a victim of the Mauve Decade, forgotten today, but who has a place in these essays as general manager of the Metropolitan Opera House from 1886 to 1891. For what more fitting symbol could there be of the Vanderbilt era than the Diamond Horseshoe? William Henry had been the prime mover in organizing and financing the company that built the new house which opened in 1883 with a performance of *Faust* starring Christine Nilsson in the role of Marguerite. Vanderbilt had not been able to obtain boxes for himself and his children in the old Academy of Music, controlled by a ring of Knickerbocker families not yet reconciled to the new money. They paid dearly for their prejudice when the academy, unable to cope with the new competition, had to close its doors three years later.

There may have been an even closer bond between the young Edmund Stanton and the Vanderbilts. According to a legend in my family he and Florence Vanderbilt (later Mrs. Twombly) may have regarded each other with a favorable eye, but any incipient romance had withered under the bleak stare of Edmund's widowed mother, who had taken the same view of the Vanderbilts as the academy boxholders. If that was so, she paid an even crueler price for her folly some two decades later when her son died, a bankrupt alcoholic at the age of forty-seven, leaving a wife and children for her to support.

Edmund had been born, however, to some affluence. His father, who also died prematurely but of a ruptured appendix, had been Daniel Drew's stockbroker. I was surprised when research uncovered this. I doubt if any of my mother's generation were even aware of it. It seemed hardly in keeping with the modest but genteel position of the family in the respectable whaling village of Stonington, Connecticut, or on the East Side of Manhattan. But a clan that avoids the headlines of history can get away with almost anything. I suppose it was perfectly possible for my great-grandfather to have bought and sold securities for old Drew and still remained honest, but one cannot but speculate that the trusted agent of so notoriously crooked a moneyman may have had to make some compromises with his conscience.

The elder Stanton left a widow, Louisa, and two sons, Edmund and my grandfather. The family was well off, but certainly not rich by the standards of the day. Edmund and Louis lived in the stylish Calumet Club and were known as fashionable young bachelors around town. Their mother made her home with a Mr. and Mrs. W. H. Tillinghast in a brownstone on Sixty-fourth Street and went with them every summer to Paris. When Mrs. Tillinghast died, and Louisa and the widower proposed to continue their summer jaunts together, her sons were constrained to point out the impropriety, despite their ages, of such a course. So, very sensibly, they married.

Tillinghast was a director of the company formed to build the new opera house, as was Louisa's nephew-in-law, George Henry Warren. When the new board, made up of magnates whose idea of music was probably thumping Verdi choruses, was looking for a secretary to mediate between it and the crazy foreigners seemingly indispensable to opera production, how could they do better than attractive, soft-spoken Ed Stanton, of supposedly artistic tastes but whom they all knew and liked, who was easily detachable from some vague insurance business and whose appointment was urged by two such stalwarts as Bill Tillinghast and Harry Warren? Edmund got the job at two thousand dollars per annum, a then-respectable salary for a man still under thirty. His first job was to raise $350,000 in bonds from the stockholders to complete the new house and to purchase the necessary paint and lumber. He must have performed his tasks efficiently, for when the first season ended badly in the red under Henry Abbey's misman- agement, and when Leopold Damrosch, summoned to substitute the cheaper-to-produce German operas for the Italian, died suddenly of pneumonia, Edmund was promoted to executive director (acting for the stockholders) and general manager of the company. This position, with its salary of fifteen thousand dollars a year, he held until 1891, when he was dismissed, aged thirty-seven, having lost the confidence of both directors and stockholders.

Walter Damrosch, who succeeded his father as conductor at the early age of twenty-three, had this to say of Edmund's appointment in his memoirs, *My Musical Life,* published some forty years later:

Curiously enough, they [the directors] appointed a young man as director of the opera, who never had any managerial or musical experience in his life. He was a relative of one of the directors and acted as Recording Secretary to the Board. He was tall, good-looking, with gentle brown eyes, always well groomed, of a kindly disposition and the most perfect and courtly manners which never failed him and which is all he had left at the end of his seven years' incumbency at which time the German opera crumbled to dust as a natural result of his curious ignorance and incompetency in matters operatic. The directors at the same time very generously appointed me as his assistant and as second conductor.

What happened?

Some time in the early months of the experimentation with German opera Edmund must have fallen in love with Wagner's music. Something in the haunting strains of *Tristan und Isolde,* in the themes of that arcane tragedy of love and death, or in the stirring motifs of the *Ring,* or in the religious ecstasy of *Parsifal* must have penetrated the polished surface of this well-mannered and obliging young man to turn him into the ardent champion of operas detested by the frivolous but powerful society of which he had once been so compliant and affable a member. For the Teutonic music dramas to which the boxholders had turned in a desperate economy move did not long hold their vagrant attention; they soon wanted more "bell songs" and less of Wotan's sepulchral vaticinations. Edmund gave all he had to the ensuing battle, and when he lost, his life simply fell apart.

But at least he had a run for his money, or rather, we should say, the boxholders'. His grandson, Sanderson Duncan, has made a record of the rise of Wagnerian performances under Edmund's management:

The initial season of opera in German, under the direction of Leopold Damrosch, featured eleven presentations, of which only three were by Wagner. Under Stanton's management the following year, four Wagnerian works were offered, and the Bayreuth composer came to assume an increasingly dominant position in the affairs of the opera house. By 1887, Stanton's third season, Wagner accounted for half of the fourteen works. In terms of the total presentations, sixty-one percent of the performances were of Wagnerian operas in that year. The season concluded with consecutive performances of the three works comprising the *Nibelungen* trilogy: *Die Walküre, Siegfried,* and *Die Götterdämmerung.* For the next three years Wagnerian receipts were to outstrip those of all other offerings by a considerable margin, in spite of an attempt of the management to include proven Italian favorites in the repertoire.

To a quarter of a million German-speaking New Yorkers the Metropolitan Opera House had now become a center of culture, and Edmund was feted and honored by the German-American clubs of the city and decorated with the Order of St. Nicholas by the Prince-Regent of Bavaria for his services "in the cause of art." He went abroad to engage singers and conductors and brought back from Germany Lilli Lehmann, Max Alvary, Emile Fischer, and Anton Seidl.

Lilli Lehmann found the house ill-equipped for the technical demands of opera and complained about the long intermissions during which stairs, barriers, benches, and other props had to be hauled in and fixed in position. Edmund placed himself at the diva's beck and call. Wearing white kid gloves, her "elegant young director," as she called him, tested the solidity of every wing on the stage and ran up and down stairs to be sure they were secure. At her suggestion he provided felt shoes for stagehands to eliminate backstage noise.

She also persuaded him to bow to the expressed wishes of his now-deceased idol and not perform *Parsifal,* which the composer had wanted produced only under very special conditions, and to pay royalties to the Wagner heirs, which had not been required by American law. On one of his trips abroad Edmund had the pleasure of handing a check to Cosima herself.

Fortified by his new passion, Edmund was becoming more assertive. At a dress rehearsal for the American premiere of *Siegfried* the tenor, Max Alvary, announced that he would spare his voice for the performance and mimic rather than sing his part. Seidl promptly called in Stanton and informed him that he would not conduct unless the tenor sang with full voice. Alvary insisted that he would sing "either today or tomorrow." "Then sing today," Stanton said curtly and left. Needless to say, Alvary did both. And one night, when the chatter in the boxes had reached a point where it was seriously curtailing the pleasure of the ticket buyers, he interrupted the performance to come out on the stage and call loudly for silence.

But it was the beginning of his end.

The revolt of the boxholders against what they considered the *longueurs* of Wagner was growing apace. Lilli Lehmann tried to warn Edmund of it; she begged him to make some concessions, but he had become stubborn. He said that the company had no voices capable of the *bel canto* required for Italian opera. He pointed out that he had had good notices from the critics, that German opera was popular with the public, and that the reputation of the opera house under the conductorship of Wagner's former secretary, Anton Seidl, had reached to all the musical capitals of Europe.

The Diamond Horseshoe was now becoming obstreperous. The *Times* chastised the boxholders for their laughter and chitchat during even the most famous arias and for the lack of courtesy of the "thirty-two-hundred-dollar ladies and gentlemen" in the parterre to the "three-dollar men and women in the orchestra stalls." Once the directors actually requested Stanton to raise the interim lights so that the persons in the boxes could better see one another during the performance. Of course, he declined to do so. One director went so far as to suggest that *Die Meistersinger* begin with its third act, "the only one with any music in it," so that he would not have to sit through the first two acts to hear it.

At last, in 1890, Stanton was forced to bow to the demands of his stockholders, and he began to look about for lighter fare to divert them. So disastrous were his experiments in this field that I cannot but wonder if there might have been an element of semi- or subconscious revenge in what he was doing, some inner compulsion to bring down a house so hostile to the great musical genius of the century. How could he have expected to please the boxholders, as he was ostensibly trying to do, with *Asrael,* by Alberti Franchetti—an Italian, it is true, but one so Wagnerized as to be considered almost a plagiarist and so inept a composer as to empty the house? Or with *Il Vassallo di Szigeth,* by Anton Smareglia, a Dalmatian, a mishmash of Hungarian sorcery and murder, dubbed by one critic "a sup of horrors"? Or, finally, with *Diana de Solange,* not only by a German but a German prince, Ernest II, duke of Saxe-Coburg–Gotha and brother-in-law of Queen Victoria, an opera so tedious that after two performances an enraged public had bowd-lerized *Solange* into "So *langweilig*"?

Diana had been composed in 1858 and produced only twice in the ensuing thirty-two years. The musical press could explain its produc-tion by Stanton only on the theory that he had received a royal decoration from the duke (who was known to be lavish with them) on the latter's visit to New York in 1890. I don't believe it. It seems more likely to me that he may have been unduly impressed by the duke's passion for Wagner. His Royal Highness had even considered dedi-cating his opus to the master. Perhaps the master had declined the honor.

Stanton had hoped to redeem himself for these failures by pro-ducing Massenet's *Le Mage* simultaneously with its Paris premiere on March 16, 1891, but by then the blow had fallen. The exasperated directors had asked for his resignation as general manager. In a parting gesture he crammed five Wagnerian operas into the remainder of the season. The *Tribune* wrote of him, "He has written his name high among those who have labored in behalf of true musical and dramatic art and will not be forgotten."

But he has been.

Stanton, who seems now to have been financially destitute, moved to Europe where living was cheaper. His wife, the former Mary Lane, daughter of a New York importer, wandered with the children from hotel to hotel on the Continent while he looked vainly for employment in England. He became deeply depressed and started to drink heavily. My mother remembered, as a girl on a trip to England, not being allowed to accompany her parents when they called on him. In 1896, the unhappy man and his wife, who was now taking morphine, settled in Bournemouth, where they put their two sons in school. The following year Edmund had himself adjudicated a bankrupt, and in 1901 he died. His widow and children returned to New York, where Louisa Tillinghast was persuaded by my grandparents to undertake their support.

Although German opera was formally banished from the Metropoli-tan by a unanimous vote of the stockholders on January 14, 1891, it has since, of course, triumphantly and permanently (except for a brief, shameful interlude during World War I) returned.

EDITH WHARTON

Edith Wharton in literary profile.

I FULLY REALIZE that Edith Wharton would have reacted with disgust to being included in this book, but it is just her dislike of the Vanderbilt era that provides her relevance to my theme. It was not that she disliked the family itself, many if not most of whom she had known in Newport. She was fond of George, whose tenant she had been in the Rue de Varenne and with whom she had stayed at Biltmore, and I think she liked his sister-in-law, the widow of Cornelius II, who had been her lessee in the same street in Paris, though she poked mild fun at her pomposity, referring to her as "Alice, Mrs. Vanderbilt," in the style of a dowager peeress. But she scorned the opulence and extravaganza of the new rich in New York, writing to Ogden Codman in 1897: "I wish the Vanderbilts didn't retard culture so very thoroughly. They are entrenched in a sort of Thermopylae of bad taste, from which apparently no force on earth can dislodge them." This reaction, as I shall try to show, was not wholly to the advantage of her fiction.

She had this to say of Proust in *A Backward Glance*: "His greatness lay in his art, his incredible littleness in the quality of his social admirations. But in this, after all, he merely exemplified the tendency not infrequent in novelists of manners—Balzac and Thackeray among them—to be dazzled by contact with the very society they satirize. If it is true that *pour comprendre il faut aimer* this seeming inconsistency may, in some, be a deep necessity of the creative imagination."

It was certainly not so of her own. For Edith Wharton's dislike of the society into which she was born and in which she spent much of the first half of her life, the society that gave her the material for that portion of her fiction that has made her famous, was so intense as to

153

have been a contributing factor to her expatriation. Her life in Europe, it is true, provided the inspiration of many fine books—she was incapable of writing a bad one—but it was far from the perfect setting for her genius.

Born in New York in 1862, Edith Newbold Jones was related or connected to everybody in Knickerbocker society: Rhinelanders, Schermerhorns, Gallatins, Stevenses, Ruthurfurds, a family network far too large and too important to be able to ignore, or even too long to disdain, the rise of the great post–Civil War mercantile and financial fortunes. Any potential conflict between the old and new was soon drowned in merger, with the happy common denominator of greed: a granddaughter of Commodore Vanderbilt married a grandson of General Washington's aide-de-camp; the son of Darius Ogden Mills, a Forty-niner, married a Livingston. And a bright-eyed, precocious young lady, spending her winters in Manhattan and her summers in Newport, took in every phase of this evolution, noting each detail of the evolving social scene: the calls, the cards, the arbitrary and inconsistent rules of inclusion and exclusion, the aping of European manners and customs, the ultimate triumph of the purse.

Edith saw it all, and she saw it as drama. But unlike Proust or Thackeray, she was never in the least dazzled by it, not even by the most dazzling Vanderbilt ball. And when she married at twenty-three she showed a certain contempt for the standards of the day, for she picked neither an old New Yorker nor a new, but an amiable nobody, a Bostonian of little means, one Edward Wharton, thirteen years older than herself, of respectable but undistinguished background, with whom she was not even in love. Perhaps she wished only to get away from an unsympathetic mother and, wed to a man with no occupation, to enjoy long trips to Europe where she could study and appreciate the beautiful aspects of an older and more dignified civilization.

To Europe, at any rate, she went, and, studying its great houses and palaces with a keen decorator's eye which soon became a professional one, she placed her finger on just what was wrong with the way in which the Vanderbilts and their ilk had attempted to bring the glories of the Renaissance and the eighteenth century to Fifth Avenue and Newport. Their plunder of the Old World had resulted in "a labyrinth of dubious eclecticism" and a fatal division of labor between architecture and house decoration. The only remedy was to go back from "the gilded age of decoration" to "the golden age of architecture," where the house and its contents were considered as a unit, and to spread her doctrine she wrote, in collaboration with the architect, Ogden Codman, *The Decoration of Houses.*

The authors illustrated their book with photographs of the interiors of such splendid edifices as Versailles, Fontainebleau, Chantilly, and the ducal palaces of Urbino, Mantua, and Florence. Why not? If the Vanderbilts wanted palaces, shouldn't they do it right?

It was quite frankly a book for millionaires. The authors take for granted a classic taste and twenty servants. Hear them on dining rooms: "Concerning the state dining room that forms a part of many modern houses little remains to be said beyond the descriptions already given of the various gala apartments. It is obvious that the banqueting-hall should be less brilliant than a ball-room and less fanciful in decoration than a music room: a severer and more restful treatment naturally suggests itself, but beyond this no special indications are required."

One can see why Edmund Wilson dubbed her not only the pioneer but the poet of interior decoration. It is easy to smile at some of the pointers in *The Decoration of Houses,* but there was a need for them in that florid day.

The great thing about the book was that it got Edith Wharton into print between hard covers. Before then she had appeared only in periodicals. Two years later she published a volume of short stories, *The Greater Inclination,* and thereafter until her death a book appeared almost annually.

Henry James, who met her and read her when she was in her late thirties, immediately saw both her problem and her danger. She had just the right knowledge and talent to "do" contemporary New York and its antecedents, and she must at all costs, he sternly warned her sister-in-law, be "tethered in native pastures, even if it reduces her to a backyard in New York." The miracle was that Edith took his advice, at least for a time. But she still had her doubts. The difficulty, as she put it, was "how to extract from such a subject the typical human significance which is the story-teller's reason for telling one story rather than another," and the answer, she at last concluded, was "that a frivolous society can acquire dramatic significance only through what its frivolity destroys." The happy result, in 1905, of this deliberation was her greatest novel, *The House of Mirth.*

But of course! Was that not what Yonville did to Emma Bovary? Or even what St. Petersburg did to Anna Karenina? Have frivolous societies not always been meat and drink to novelists? Perhaps Edith felt that New York was unduly shallow, lacking the more venerable shallowness of European cities. At any rate, it was eight years before she made it the principal subject of another novel. *The Custom of the Country* is certainly one of her most powerful books, perhaps a trifle marred by the very violence of her attack on the new rich. She allows her disdain for their crudeness to appear, something Flaubert never does. He simply reveals his burghers for what they are.

From 1913 until her death in 1937 Edith resided in France, and she gradually lost touch with her native city. When New York now appeared in her fiction, it was simply the setting and no longer the point of the drama, and her settings changed more and more to Europe. Only when she placed characters in the now-distant past did the old society of her childhood reappear as an integral part of their story. The horrors of the First World War and the deterioration of manners that succeeded it caused her to look back on the quaint, staid, ordered city of the eighteen-seventies with a nostalgia purged of her earlier acerbities. As she relates in her memoirs: "When I was young it used to seem to me that the group in which I grew up was like an empty vessel into which no new wine would ever again be poured. Now I see that one of its uses lay in preserving a few drops of an old vintage too rare to be savoured by a youthful palate."

Out of this new and gentler mood grew *The Age of Innocence* (1920), the four novelettes that make up *Old New York,* and, in her last year, the unfinished *The Buccaneers.* I have no doubt that Henry James would have approved of these, which are certainly among the finest of her work. If she had not followed his injunction to tether herself in native pastures, at least she had known how to recapture them.

In sharp contrast to the quiet and peace with which Edith chose to bathe the memory of her early years was the frenetic pace of her social and sight-seeing life in Europe. Sometimes, particularly on her jaunts to England, her cultivation of titled folk and her visits to historic houses seemed to belie her supposed lack of interest in the purely social scene. Of course she might have retorted that something of what was finest in French and English culture was distilled in the graceful life of the old nobility in beautiful, venerable habitations, linking the centuries in a golden chain of tradition. She might have insisted that she cared only for cultivated aristocrats and that she had no more use for dreary peers than she did for dreary peasants. And she would have been to some extent correct. But then Proust sought to explain his passion for French titles as an interest in French history. Snobbishness is an insidious thing. As one succumbs to the lure of beautiful possessions, of parks and gardens, doesn't one tend to magnify the intellectual attainments of their owners? A duchess of Towers may pass a test that a Mrs. Smith would fail. Edith herself said of the man she most admired, Henry James, that he was one part angel, one part genius, and one part Major Pendennis. Proust and Thackeray were fortunate in that their bedazzlement was with the society that became their natural habitat. Edith Wharton's was with one that, however minutely observed, was not innately her own.

Her own, furthermore, she rejected even more strongly as time passed. If she had reversed her strictures of the New York of her childhood there was no such mercy for the contemporary metropolis. Indeed, she extended her distaste for it to the whole nation. A recent edition of her letters again and again strikes this shrill note. Here is her opinion, in 1904, of a summer hotel in Petersham, Massachusetts: "I despair of the Republic! Such dreariness, such whining, sallow women, such utter absence of the amenities, such crass food, crass manners, crass landscape! And mind you, it is a new and fashionable hotel. What a horror it is for a whole nation to be developing without the sense of beauty and eating bananas for breakfast."

Two decades later, when Mrs. Winthrop Chanler protested that Edith was going too far in her distaste for her native land and offered Ethel Derby (Theodore Roosevelt's daughter) as the example of a great woman who was also innately American, Edith replied tartly: "You mustn't lecture me for not appreciating America on the score that I don't know Ethel Derby, for I've known her for years and like her very much. . . . Of course there are green isles in that sea of misery."

One writer who observed his friend Edith perhaps more keenly than any of her other intimates and who questioned the value to her writing of her multifold social activities was Percy Lubbock. He was (for a long time, anyway) one of her small court of English intellectual, upper-class, perhaps a bit epicene bachelors, but he was also a critic and author of the first class, though of a small output. After Edith's death he collected the reminiscences of her friends and wove them together into the charming and deeply perceptive *Portrait of Edith Wharton,* published in 1947. It was greeted, however, with mixed reactions.

Even literary scholars succumb at times to the temptation of becoming "fans" of their subjects, and Lubbock's book aroused considerable resentment among Wharton's devotees for his supposed denigration of her. I disagree that it is that, but let me admit right off that Lubbock labored under what many biographers would consider a disqualification. Edith Wharton, who was very possessive about her men friends, had not been able to forgive him his marriage to Lady Sybil Desart.

Lady Sybil, one must admit, made it hard for Edith. As her daughter, Iris Origo, once put it to me, she had married, in seemingly rapid succession, three of Edith's most cherished bachelors: Bayard Cutting, Geoffrey Scott, and finally Percy, who had reached an age where Edith had deemed him "safe." This had proved the last straw, and after a few tense scenes she and Percy had given up seeing each other. Why then did he consider himself the man to paint her posthumous portrait?

Because, as he said to one critic, "I adored her!" She had been one of the great things in his life, and now that she was dead and his wife a hopeless invalid, he must have felt that he would be able to reconsider the past without rancor. Furthermore, though one of the finest prose writers of his day, he always suffered from a paucity of material that he considered just right for his talent. His remembered work consists of two short novels, some criticism, studies of Eton, and of his family's country house in Norfolk—and Edith Wharton. He could not afford to give her up.

We should remember that his title is *Portrait* of Edith Wharton, and that is just what it is. It is not, as he states in his preface, a biography or a review of her fiction. Percy used his words with precision. When Iris Origo once remarked that he seemed never to cross out a word, he replied, "I *think* before I write." He has limned Edith as she appears to the world and to her intimates, in her garden, in her drawing room, in the backseat of her Panhard speeding through Italian hill towns, at parties, in big groups, in small groups, disciplined, neat, sharp, giving herself up to high trills of laughter or to freezing frowns, imperious, impossible, spoiled, but also generous, self-deprecating, reaching out passionately to friends and then pulling suddenly back in fear of being intrusive or misunderstood. Those who suppose that Lubbock was hard on her do not realize how many people disliked or were put off by Edith Wharton. The combination of her shyness with her impatience made her very brusque at times, and she never suffered fools gladly. I have little doubt that most of her contemporary acquaintances (as opposed to her friends) found Lubbock's portrait highly complimentary. And certainly the vision he evokes is of a brilliant and fascinating woman.

A more serious criticism of Lubbock's book is that it underrates her fiction. It is true that he speaks of some "ingenuous" people supposing that her books had to be written "on the bare margin of such a populous and ornamental existence," and he goes on to imply that a greater concentration on her art might have yielded greater results. Here is how he imagines Edith's relationship to her muse: "Well, I only mean, after all, that when she sat at her work, she faced a companion whom she loved and trusted, but one who never was, never had the chance to be, all the comfort and cheer that she required. Her companion, I could fancy, had no illusions on this head—but may have thought he could have done more for her all the same, first and last, than she was willing to believe."

It is not to denigrate her work to say that it could have been better. Percy's standards were of the very highest; his *The Craft of Fiction* deals only with the greatest novelists. Of course he did not rate her as high as he did Henry James, whom he regarded as the master and whose posthumous editor he became, but Edith, who was uncharacteristically modest about her own claims to literary survival, would have been pleased with this evaluation of her characters:

Look, then, at her books, and with a swift glance consider the assembly of men and women, of all ages and various conditions, who crowd the field of her twenty or thirty novels. A vigorous crowd it is, and among them are many, the most assured, the most confident of all in their reality, of whom you may ask where on earth, with her exclusive preferences, she had learned to know them; but of course it was not on earth that she had known or had need to know them, she had divined them in flashes, in glimpses, keen and full enough for the curiosity, the brisk-eyed irony and humor of so busily creative a brain.

Lubbock is saying that her genius could make good use of very little. True, but it could make even more of much. A few glimpses might give her Ethan Frome, but a lifetime had given her Lily Bart. Which brings me back, precisely, to the world of her original observations and experiences, the New York society that, as she herself had put it, she had had "to hand," but which she had abandoned for Europe. Certainly "so busily creative a brain" could find the material needed for the fiction it had to produce all over the world, but a wide range is not necessarily a boon to an artist. The drab ugliness of brownstone Manhattan and the chilly order of its limited society may have driven her to seek greater beauty in England, Italy, and France, but the lovely château of Givré in *The Reef* is not so vivid as Mrs. Peniston's cluttered Fifth Avenue parlor in *The House of Mirth*. Jane Austen's confinement to a few villages in the south of England and Emily Brontë's to one in the north may be deemed literary advantages compared to Edith's constant "motor flights" to sites of greater and greater picturesqueness. These latter were of indubitable assistance in the writing of her admirable travel books, but they added only a few attractive frills to her fiction.

The romantic love that she found abroad was of as modest a use to the novelist as the beautiful settings. Edith, speaking of love in her letters, in her books, in her quoted conversations, and, worst of all, in her poetry, was inclined to be high-toned, lofty, synthetic, even a touch phony, the very opposite of her best, down-to-earth, very funny side. After more than twenty years of a sexless marriage she had the misfortune to fall in love with Morton Fullerton, an apparently charming but certainly weak-charactered and self-centered minor journalist, somewhat her junior, who seemed always to be trying to extricate himself from the tangles of love affairs he had been too soft to avoid and who was perfectly willing to use Edith's money to keep one of his more persistent mistresses from publishing a collection of his love letters to various persons of both sexes. Of course, he soon tired of the demanding and passionate great lady of letters he had been proud enough to add to his list, and poor Edith had to learn the humiliation of discovering that her proud faith that she would never try to hold a man beyond the period of his inclination was the merest bluff.

She had written to Fullerton in the first happy days of their affair that, when the end came, he was simply to put her letters in a bundle and send them back, and that she would understand. But when that time came it was not so easy. "What has brought about such a change?" she wailed. "Oh, no matter what it is—*only tell me!* . . . My reason rejects the idea that a man like you, who has felt a warm sympathy for a woman like me, can suddenly, from one day to another, without any act or word on her part, lose even a friendly regard for her, and discard the mere outward signs of consideration by which friendship speaks."

At last she was able to write him: "The tiresome woman is *buried*, once for all, I promise, and only the novelist survives. *Viens déjeuner avec elle sans crainte demain.*" It is never pleasant to contemplate a superior person in the emotional grip of a more flawed soul.

So great, however, is the romantic faith of Academia in the power of Venus, so determined are biographers to find a great love for every literary genius, a Robert Browning for every Elizabeth Barrett, that the discovery of the Fullerton-Wharton affair was acclaimed by critics. It was even said that Edith's nature had found fulfillment at last and that a deeper note was thereafter to be detected in her fiction. No such claim was made by the novelist herself, who wrote to Fullerton at the end of the affair, "My life was better before I knew you." The only book of hers that seems to contain the description of a night with Fullerton, *The Reef,* is one of her palest and most contrived (Henry James called it "Racinian"), and her finest work, *The House of Mirth,* was written before the harried, blackmailed journalist ever appeared on her scene.

And now let us suppose for a moment a scenario more likely than the one that occurred. For was it credible that Edith Jones, an attractive and brilliant young woman of wealth and the best connections, should have allied herself to an impecunious Bostonian, with neither trade nor future, more than a dozen years older than herself, with whom she was not even in love? Surely it was more in the cards that she would pick a competent New Yorker, adequately sexual, probably a lawyer, with a future ahead of him, and settle down to a life of raising children and writing. Yes, writing. Why not? New York society, it is true, might still have bored her, but with a husband she loved who was getting ahead (perhaps a kind of Newland Archer), sons to be educated, and daughters to be brought out, it would have fallen into place in her life. And think what the author of *The House of Mirth* might have had to say about the New England boarding schools, about Yale and Harvard, about the roaring twenties, the Great Depression, and the advent of the New Deal!

But I am playing games. Let us be grateful for the fine novels we have. Anyone who wishes to know Edith Wharton as deeply as she can be known to date should read three books: R. W. B. Lewis's biography, Lubbock's *Portrait,* and her own memoirs, *A Backward Glance.*

Iris Origo, stepdaughter of Lubbock and the distinguished author of books on Leopardi and Byron, has described a weekend on Long Island that Edith spent with Iris's American grandmother, Mrs. Bayard Cutting, on the novelist's last trip to her native land to receive an honorary degree from Yale. It is one of the rare recorded occasions when the survivor from New York's age of innocence predominated over the international figure of perfect houses and gardens. Iris relates how Edith refused to be led into any discussion of persons or events in France, of Carlo Placi or Madame de Noailles, and how, at each such attempt, she gently and firmly steered the conversation back to old friends and old memories in New York. W's house on Eleventh Street, had it really been pulled down? Did her hostess remember the night they had dined there before the Colony Club ball? X's daughter, the fair one, had she married her young Bostonian? Had Z indeed lost all his money?

"For the whole evening, this mood continued. At one moment only—as, the last guest gone, she turned half-way up the stairs to wave good-night—I caught a glimpse of the other Edith: elegant, formidable, as hard and dry as porcelain. Then, as she looked down on her old friends, her face softened, even the erectness of her spine relaxed a little. She was no longer the trim, hard European hostess, but a nice old American lady. Edith had come home."

HENRY ADAMS
AND
HIS BROTHERS

Mrs. Hugh Hammersley by Sargent.

NOTHING is more commonly said of Henry Adams than that he represented a thinning of the blood of an imperial line, that lacking the qualities of leadership of his presidential grandfather and great-grandfather he elected to remain on the sidelines, standing critically aloof from the hurly-burly of the political arena and the marketplace. But Henry, as well as his brothers, Charles Francis, Jr., and Brooks, had many of the sterling qualities of John and John Quincy. Indeed, the resemblance between the generations was remarkable. What had changed was not they but the nation. No Adams could have been elected President of the United States in the last half of the nineteenth century because no Adams was ever capable of courting public favor. It might also be said that no Adams was capable of making a dirty deal.

In a Vanderbilt era Henry and his brothers felt strikingly out of place. Henry claimed he was less equipped for life in America in the nineteenth century than had he been born a Polish Jew or "a furtive Yacoob and Ysacc still reeking of the Ghetto, snarling a weird Yiddish to the officers of the customs." Politicians were corrupt and businessmen unscrupulous. But the Adamses did not therefore turn their backs on a world of which they understandably disapproved. Instead they became such successful critics of it that they are more remembered today than the senators and tycoons whom they had deemed better adapted.

Charles Francis, Jr., was the one who stood least aloof. As John C. Meleney has said of him: "His life spanned the Gilded Age, and he was in it if not entirely of it. He was ambivalent concerning the materialistic orientation of his time, clearly enjoying wealth and the good life, seeking and grasping opportunities to invest for profit, but critical of those whom he considered mere money getters and traders." Three-quarters of his autobiography, which appeared in 1916, the year following that of his death, is devoted to his early life and to the Civil War in which he was actively engaged as a cavalry officer. He makes no bones of the fact that he fiercely enjoyed the many battles he fought against what he considered an arrogant and fire-eating foe. "Never on this earth," he observed, "did human beings more richly deserve the complete, out-and-out thrashing that those men then coveted and afterwards had."

Charles was perhaps the gruffest member of a family of whom Charles Eliot Norton said, "The Adamses have a genius for saying even a gracious thing in an ungracious manner." Henry Adams retorted to a young man who ventured to compliment him on his older brother's manner, "You found Charles charming? You interest me!" But behind the gruffness lay an absolute loyalty to friends and family, a high sense of honor and public duty, a dry wit, and a modesty tempered with realism. Charles summed up his career thus: "I now humbly thank fortune that I have almost got through life without making a conspicuous ass of myself."

In the railroad business with which he became involved after the war he perfectly saw that "Caesarism" would not do, that the Vanderbilts and their ilk were wreckers as well as builders, and that regulation was essential, and he served for a long and conscientious term as chairman of the Massachusetts Board of Railroad Commissioners. But when he went into active railroad management and became a director and ultimately chairman of the board of Union Pacific, he was, in his own phrase, "wholly demoralized." "I hated my position and its duties and yearned to be free of it and them. My office had become a prison house. . . . In the course of my railroad experiences I made no friends, apart from those in the Boston direction; nor among those I met was there any man whose acquaintance I valued. They were a coarse, realistic, bargaining crowd."

He was finally ejected from the board of Union Pacific by Jay Gould, and there have been those who have purported to see in this the superior strength and vigor of the new enterpreneur over the Back Bay aristocrat. But this is absurd. The man who avoided service in the war to lay the foundation stones of his fraudulently built empire was hardly stronger or more vigorous than the cavalry colonel, the Massachusetts railroad commission chairman, and the managing stockholder of a Kansas City stockyard which Charles developed into a multi-million-dollar enterprise. It was simply that Gould would stoop to things that an Adams would not, and that the era declined to police the Goulds. In a lawless community crime is bound to pay.

Charles's brother Henry's disgust with the plutocracy of the age, embracing not only its methods of accumulating wealth but its conspicuous consumption of it, was even fiercer than that of his older sibling. It did not, however, with Henry, become a near obsession until his middle years. Up to the age of forty-seven Henry might have reasonably considered that his life was a happy and successful one. He had not, to be sure, been President of the United States, or even a minister to England, like his father, but he had been an innovative teacher of medieval history at Harvard, almost a cult among the more brilliant undergraduates, and a provocative editor of the *North American Review;* and he was in the process of completing his nine-volume history of the Jefferson and Madison administrations which, for all his deprecation of it, has become a classic. But more important than all this was his marriage to Marian "Clover" Adams. As he told one of his nieces, "I met only one woman in my life I wanted to marry, and I married her."

And then, on December 6, 1885, fate "smashed the life out of him." Clover, whose family had a history of suicidal depressions, took a fatal dose of potassium cyanide. She had adored her husband, perhaps as deeply as he her, and their very childlessness had proved a further bond, but nothing had been able to pull her out of the black depression triggered by her father's death.

Henry had always been a man of few intimacies. "One friendship in a life is much," he wrote; "two are many; three are hardly possible." Certainly his two were Clarence King, the geologist, and John Hay, the biographer of Lincoln and later secretary of state. But I doubt that Henry, who used a sharp wit and a gruff, kindly cynicism as a barrier to and possibly a substitute for the closest human communion, ever revealed his deepest emotions or thoughts to any but Clover. She had been quick-witted, even caustic, but blessed with gaiety and an exquisite sensitivity. She and Henry, in Washington, where they had settled, had been able to laugh cheerfully enough together at "goldbugs" and politicians without getting overwrought at the scandals of the capital of which he made amusing use in his novel *Democracy*. Henry James had pictured them as the socially exclusive but good-humored Bonnycastles in *Pandora,* where the husband, finding at the end of the season that his wife may have been a bit too choosy, exclaims, "Hang it, there's only a month left, let us be vulgar and have some fun—let us invite the President!"

But now, without Clover, everything palled. After the first stunning shock of his grief Henry went doggedly back to work to finish his history. This done, at fifty-two, he announced that his life was over and that like a worn-out race horse he could be turned out to pasture. In the summer of 1890, he plucked the glad-to-be-plucked painter John La Farge from the bosom of his large family to take him off on a voyage of indefinite duration to the South Seas.

The Pacific opened up a new dimension of color. La Farge taught Henry to observe the clearness of the butterfly blue of the sky, the varieties of pink and lilac and purple and rose in the clouds at sunset. In Samoa the natives, grave and courteous, greeted them benevolently, and they drank the ceremonial *kawa* and watched the *siva,* a dance performed by girls, seated cross-legged, naked to the waist, their dark skins shining with coconut oil. It was a world where instinct was everything, where Henry, the author of two anonymous novels, began at last to allow the long-repressed aesthete in his nature to predominate over the strictly disciplined historian.

Much as he admired La Farge's watercolors, he felt that his friend had not quite caught the expression for the islands. "His hard work over studied compositions is interesting, but it does not much interest me because I have seen the original subjects and know how little of them can be put on paper or panel. I cannot get expression for the South Seas. Languor that is not languid; voluptuousness that is not voluptuous; a poem without poetry."

Some years later he put into a privately printed book what he had learned of the history of Tahiti from his conversations with the old ex-queen Hinari (or Grandmother). But *The Memories of Arii Taima* is something of a bore. Tahiti had no history in the Western sense of the word; there is nothing but genealogy and legend. Yet the writing of these memoirs marked an important step in Henry's evolution to artist. The day was coming when he would find a subject that required not

168

only meticulous research but the imagination of the man who had sat on the floor of the old queen's hut and listened as she intoned the poems of her family tradition. *Mont-Saint-Michel and Chartres* is a unique tour de force of the artistic imagination; its language shimmers with the magic blue of the windows of the great cathedral. Once, at the Metropolitan Museum of Art, gazing at the "Orana Maria," I found myself wondering if Adams's Virgin of Chartres, like Gauguin's Virgin of the Pacific, might not owe something to the colors and legends of the South Seas.

Looking into the question, I discovered that Gauguin had arrived in Tahiti only a few days after Adams and La Farge had left, and I speculated that Adams might have agreed with me that the French artist had caught precisely what he had felt was the elusive expression of the area, the voluptuousness that was not voluptuous, the poem that was not poetry. But there is no record, so far as I know, that Henry ever saw a painting by Gauguin. Certainly La Farge would not have tempted him to look for one. The latter, long afterwards, wrote Henry about an illustrated catalogue of a Gauguin show in Paris. He informed his former traveling companion that the "mad Frenchman," who had been in Tahiti after their visit, was a sorry failure as an artist, desperately trying to catch the attention of a novelty-hunting public. Ah, well. We know that Southey told Charlotte Brontë to go back to her knitting needles and that André Gide declined to publish *Swann's Way*.

Henry had insisted that his career as a writer was over. "I have said and stick to it that I will never again appear as an author," he wrote John Hay. He might write anonymously, but "of course I should not touch the South Seas; I could not without betraying myself." In fact, as we have seen, the greatest phase of his literary career was beginning. But first he would have his vision, on a visit to the Chicago World's Fair in 1893, of the epitome of all that to him was most pernicious in the world created by and for the "goldbug." Reminding Hay of what we have already heard him say of Sargent's "Mrs. Hammersley," he wrote:

Do you remember Sargent's portrait of Mrs. Hammersley in London this summer? Was it a defiance or an insult to our society, or a rendering in good faith of our civilization, or a conscious snub to French and English art, or an unconscious revelation of the artist's despair of reconciliation with the female of the goldbug? I say the female, because the male has been the butt of the artist for generations. Well, the Chicago Architecture is precisely an architectural Mrs. Hammersley. I like to look at it as an appeal to the human animal, the superstitious and ignorant savage within us, that has instincts and no reason, against the world as money has made it. I have seen a faint gleam of intelligence lighten the faces even of the ignorant rich, and almost penetrate the eyes of a mugwump and Harvard College graduate, as he brooded, in his usual stolidity of self-satisfaction, on his own merits, before the Court of Honor.

I take it that Henry is saying that the architects of the fair's pompous structures, like Sargent, have succeeded, perhaps unintentionally, in mocking their own creations, so that the unspoiled savage beneath the surface of any man (the Samoan?) is alerted to the basic folly of a false civilization. But an even more violent diatribe would be offered to Hay a month later: "The goldbugs have undertaken to ruin things, and have already shown such incompetence, terror and greed that nothing but disaster can come of it. I would pardon them their rascality on the stock exchange and their imbecility in politics, but I can't forgive them their massacre of my friends who are being cleaned out and broken down by dozens."

He wanted to massacre "the whole Knickerbocker Club." But in the summer of 1895, traveling with Senator Henry Cabot Lodge of Massachusetts and his family in Normandy (Lodge, one of his students at Harvard, had been a lifelong friend), he had a new revelation of himself in history and a glimmer of what he might do with it. He found himself unexpectedly happy over the stones that his "respectable Norman ancestors" had carved and piled up: Caen, Bayeux, Saint-Lô, Coutances, and Mont-Saint-Michel.

With the Renaissance, the Valois and the Tudor display, I can have nothing to do. It leaves me admiring but cold. With true Norman work, the sensation is that of personal creation. No doubt Amiens and Chartres are greatly superior architecture, but I was not there. I was a vassal of the Church; I held farms—for I was many—in the Cotentin and around Caen, but the thing I did by a great majority of ancestors was to help in building the Cathedral of Coutances, and my soul is still built into it. I can almost remember the faith that gave me energy, and the sacred boldness that made my towers seem to me so daring, with the bits of gracefulness that I hazarded with some doubts whether the divine grace could be properly shown outside. Within I had no doubts. There the contrite sinner was welcomed with such tenderness as makes me still wish I were one. There is not a stone in the whole interior which I did not treat as though it were my own child. I was not clever, and I made some mistakes which the great men of Amiens corrected. I was simple-minded, somewhat stiff and cold, almost repellent to the warmer natures of the south, and I had lived always where one fought handily and needed to defend one's wives and children; but I was at my best. Nearly eight hundred years have passed since I made the fatal mistake of going to England, and since then I have never done anything in the world that can begin to compare in the perfection of its spirit and art with my cathedral of Coutances. I am as sure of it as I am of death.

Henry's vision in Normandy is comparable to Gibbon's on the steps of the Ara Coeli where he conceived the plan of *The Decline and Fall.* It was the germ that grew up to his two great books, *Mont-Saint-Michel and Chartres* and *The Education of Henry Adams,* evocations of the thirteenth century, when he would have liked to have lived, and the twentieth, in which he reluctantly found himself, a contrast of worlds of unity and multiplicity, of order and chaos.

Henry was perfectly conscious of the fact that he had become an artist; indeed he now saw art as the only way of communicating serious thought. Didacticism had to be eschewed; moralizing disguised. As he wrote to Cabot Lodge's son, the poet Bay: "How are you going to grab me by the throat, after the strenuous presidential manner, and jam your pill down? That is the whole subject of dispute. That is art." A storyteller, he maintained, had to be "a trivial sort of animal who amuses me"; his first quality should be superficiality. It was why he vastly preferred Jane Austen to George Eliot. Toward the end of his life he wrote to Barrett Wendell that narrative and didactic purpose could never be mixed, which was where he (Adams) and Saint Augustine and Rousseau had all partially failed. And indeed, if he was referring to the late chapters of *The Education,* where he went hopelessly astray in applying the laws of physics to human events, he is correct. But in art, anyway, he had found something that transcended his deepest pessimism.

It also gave him a needed distraction from his constant preoccupation with the evils of the goldbugs of the Vanderbilt era. Incidentally, he did not carry his animus to individuals. He was a close friend of a daughter of James G. Blaine, one of the famously corrupt politicians of the day, and a friend of Cornelius Vanderbilt II, William K., and George.

Brooks, the youngest of the Adams brothers, arrives on their austere scene as a bit of an anticlimax, even as something of a caricature. It may not have been only his harsh manner and incessant disputatiousness that exasperated his brother Henry, but his constant cries of doom, which may have struck the latter as an almost ribald takeoff of his own pose as the worldly wise and world-weary seer, what he sometimes called "the old cardinal." In the words of their niece, Abigail Adams Homans, one of the few persons who ever succeeded in loving Brooks, the latter "was a violent and savage man—brusque, intolerant, opinionated, cranky and tactless to the last degree—but in spite of these idiosyncrasies he was at bottom warm-hearted and infinitely loyal."

He was also a complete medievalist. He approved of the subjugation of women and opposed their being given the franchise. He extolled the virtues of the martial man and the convent-bred woman. As Abigail put it, "He was like a child in his love for the fighting man." Small wonder that Theodore Roosevelt found him sympathetic!

Brooks set himself up as the archenemy of the goldbug to whose machinations his writings ascribed the fall of all the great civilizations. In *The Law of Civilization and Decay* he developed the determinist theory that any historical era or empire has only a given amount of energy which is bound to be used up in human competition. The originally separate units of the empire are drawn together by a force of centralization which intensifies as power is converted from the weapons of warfare to currency. In the beginning, for example, society is made up of agricultural units which come to be united by conquest, ushering in the age of the warrior, the martial age, which, needless to say, was to Brooks the high point of culture and art. But continued centralization favors the big city, and in the crowded metropolis the usury class soon learns to dominate the military. Here is how Brooks saw the decline of Rome:

"The administration of Augustus organized the permanent police. . . . A body of wage earners, drawn from the ends of the earth, was made cohesive by money. For more than four hundred years this corps of hirelings crushed revolt within the empire. . . . But a time came when the suction of the usurers so wasted the life of the community that the stream of bullion ceased to flow from the capital to the frontiers; then, as the sustaining force failed, the line of troops along the Danube and the Rhine was drawn out until it broke, and the barbarians poured in unchecked."

Although American civilization is not covered in *The Law,* Brooks obviously believed it was well down the road of decay, lost in the viselike grip of the money-jugglers. To him the Vanderbilt era was the epitome of the vulgar, the nonheroic. The usurer was now god; Shylock was entitled not only to his pound of flesh, but to all the blood its excision might entail. My citation of Shylock is deliberate, for Brooks had no hestitation in identifying Jews with the most grasping of usurers. It is sad to relate that his brother Henry suffered from the same prejudice and delusion. It is an undoubted blot on the escutcheon of a great artist and historian.

Brooks's description of the state of British society in 1895 has an odd relevance to New York of the same period:

The advent of portraiture has usually been considered to portend decay, and rightly, since the presence of the portrait demonstrates the supremacy of wealth. A portrait can hardly be the ideal of an enthusiast, like the figure of a god, for it is a commercial article, sold for a price, and manufactured to suit a patron's taste; were it made to please the artist, it might not find a buyer. . . . This mercenary quality forms the gulf which has divided the art of the middle ages from that of modern times—a gulf which cannot be bridged, and which has broadened with the lapse of centuries, until at last the artist, like all else in society, has become the creature of a commercial market, even as the Greek was sold as a slave to the plutocrat of Rome. With each invention, with each acceleration of movement, prose has more completely supplanted poetry, while the economic intellect has grown less tolerant of any departure from those representations of nature which have appealed to the most highly gifted of the monied type among successive generations. Hence the imperiousness of modern realism. . . . In an economic period, like that which has followed the Reformation, wealth is the form in which energy seeks expression: therefore, since the close of the fifteenth century, architecture has reflected money. . . . The architecture, the sculpture, and the coinage of London at the close of the nineteenth century, when compared with those of the Paris of Saint Louis, recall the Rome of Caracalla as contrasted with the Athens of Pericles.

Brooks was always an extremist, and at times an absurd one, but I suppose adherents of his theory (if he had any) could find some support in the portraits of Sargent, the sculpture of Saint-Gaudens, and the massive mansions of Richard Morris Hunt. And what would Brooks have said of the rich art patrons of our own time, some of whom buy abstract paintings and kinetic sculpture, live in glass houses, and have themselves painted in the nude? But of course he would have cited them as his ultimate proof! Did they not represent the disintegration of society that must follow the era of economic centralization just as surely as the latter had to follow the age of imagination and faith?

Louis C. Tiffany
and
Stanford White

The "Vanderbilt portal" by Stanford White,
Saint Bartholomew's Church, New York City.
SAMUEL H. GOTTSCHO

TIFFANY & CO., which celebrated its one hundred and fiftieth anniversary in 1987, played a role in moderating the increasingly flamboyant tastes of the post–Civil War decades somewhat analogous to that of our Supreme Court in the development of constitutional law. One of the most vital functions of that tribunal is to act as a brake on social reform, even necessary social reform, to keep it from coming too fast and from treading too heavily on civil and property rights that in the long run may be more compatible with it than may first appear. Liberal opinion is inclined to want too much too soon, and time is needed for the appropriate legislation to be worked out. Yet when that has happened, and the court modifies, or even reverses, its earlier opinions, there still remains an aura of stability that lends force and dignity to our concept of law.

Similarly, Tiffany's has achieved its position in the history of American taste by refusing to give in to every fad and fancy for the sake of a fast buck, yet has been willing to adapt itself in the long run to any fundamental change of manners.

Charles Tiffany, the founder of the store and its proprietor for sixty-five years (a period that almost exactly coincided with the reign of Queen Victoria), came of modest but secure Colonial stock. His grandfather had been a farmer in Massachusetts and his father the owner of a textile mill in Connecticut. They were upright, conscientious men, and Charles in his long business career never descended to the financial chicanery so common to the age. When he became rich, as he did even by robber baron standards (he left an estate in 1902 of forty million), he continued to live simply, at least by Vanderbilt standards. He showed no tendency to be dazzled by the strutting of Fifth Avenue and Newport. Yet he knew the social world backward and forward; he knew the parvenus and the old families, and he knew how thin were the borders that divided them. In Tiffany diamonds the Colonel's lady and Rosie O'Grady were on their way to becoming sisters over the skin.

If the Tiffanys could be likened to the Medici, Louis Comfort Tiffany might be to his father as Lorenzo il Magnifico was to Cosimo Pater Patriae. Charles was the great administrator, the sober, solid founder of the feast. Louis was the artist and art patron, the imaginative genius, but never a manager, never a conserver. When he died in 1932, he left only a small fraction of the fortune bequeathed to him by his father. Yet if one owned today that same fraction of the objects Louis Tiffany designed and made, one would be rich indeed. The name Tiffany owes its fame equally to father and son.

Charles understandably wanted his son to go into the store, but he was a loving parent, willing to support his children in any life work that they seriously elected, and he had soon to acknowledge that the boy who hated schoolwork and preferred to play with colored pebbles and bits of broken glass picked up on the beach during Montauk summers had better be allowed to skip college and study painting, so Louis went to Paris. He showed a real talent almost at once—his "Duane Street" anticipated the work of the Ashcan School by almost thirty years—but he nonetheless ultimately decided that his true gift was for design and decoration, and he gave up painting to form the Tiffany Studios, which, although legally independent of Tiffany & Co., used the store as an outlet for many of its products, including glassware. Louis also became an officer of the store, so his proud father had him, after all, in a family business.

He was in every way the opposite of his sire—tall, dashing, handsome, with a reddish brown beard and mustache and eyes that always seemed to be laughing. Although he put in long days at the studio, he was able at night to cut a fashionable figure in the social circles of the town. Nor did he limit himself to Fifth Avenue; in 1870 he became the youngest member elected to the Century Association, a serious intellectual club dedicated to the appreciation of arts and letters. If he had given up a career as a painter, it was to embrace one as an artist in what to him was an even broader sense of the word. He seemed determined to turn life itself into a picture, or the outside of life, anyway, the objects with which man surrounded himself. He would concern himself not only with the houses and parks that his friends and clients constructed, but with everything that went into them: the furniture, the carpets, the glass, the book bindings, the utensils, the flowers, all that fell into the widest range of the word "decoration." And with a shining new skin, might not his old world find a new soul?

Louis had discovered the principle that Edith Wharton and Ogden Codman would later enunciate in *The Decoration of Houses*: that architecture and decoration should never have been allowed to fork into separate and independent professions and should be reunited, as they had been in the Renaissance. Laurelton Hall, the eighty-room mansion that he built for himself and his second wife up and down a hill in Cold Spring Harbor, New York, was unlike any dwelling that anyone had ever seen before. It was a fantastic, asymmetrical edifice in a mélange of styles, largely Moorish, with a three-story entrance hall, under a dome of Tiffany glass, containing a fountain and pool filled by a stream that ran through the ground story out to the terrace and cascaded down, from basin to basin, through a Babylonian hanging garden to Long Island Sound. Louis maintained that his inspiration had been the Grand Canyon.

Tiffany Studios decorated many famous mansions and clubs, usually in exotic styles, Oriental or Byzantine or Moorish, or sometimes simply fantastic, but always exciting and luxurious. These styles did not quite add up to Art Nouveau, but approached it, in a blend of Islamic carvings and painted friezes. Yet Louis's exoticism did not prevent him from giving the customer what he wanted. A booklet by a military organization on the decorations of his Veterans' Room in the Seventh Regiment Armory described "the clamp and clang of iron, the metallic lustres, the ponderous beams" as "all clearly and undeniably assimilable and matchable with the huge, hard, clanging ponderosities of wars and tramping regiments and armories."

Louis Tiffany's greatest work was in glass. Early in his career he determined to find a way of incorporating brilliant colors and varied texture within the glass itself, bearing in mind Ruskin's warning: "No man who knows what painting means can endure a painted glass window which emulated a painter's work." In the opinion of the art critic Herwin Schaeffer, Louis's designs were comparable to the work of Post-Impressionist painters, because the soft transitions were eliminated and the areas of color set one against the other by black leading. Tiffany windows depicted brilliantly colored, highly realistic scenes and were in great demand for homes and churches. But the reaction was to come.

I have said in earlier chapters that New York society was un-leavened by artists. Louis was one of the leaders who changed that. Sculptors, painters, and even actors mingled with the survivors and heirs of the old Four Hundred at his great costume ball in the winter of 1913, described by *The New York Times,* which should have known, having already covered the W. K. Vanderbilts' in 1883 and the Bradley Martins' in 1896, as "the most lavish costume fete ever seen in New York." Even Louis's Dutch Renaissance mansion on Madison Avenue and Seventy-second Street, which covered ten thousand square feet and stood five stories high, was not large enough for the spectacle. The guests were invited in hieroglyphics on a roll of papyrus to come to the Tiffany Studios, where the central chamber had been transformed into a replica of ancient Alexandria, sumptuously decorated for the nuptials of Antony and Cleopatra, the representation of which, complete with Ethiopian slaves, gladiators, palanquins, and Roman soldiers, would constitute the main event of the evening. The guests were certainly cooperative; they submitted their costumes for the approval of a select committee, and the popular portraitist John Alexander, who went as a mummy, was even willing to remain propped up against a wall for much of the night.

Yet for all the elaboration of their efforts they look somewhat ridiculous in the photographs so profusely taken. I knew an old French lady, a survivor of the era, who coined a term for such goings-on: "silly-clever." She claimed that it covered much of the art and literature of the time. And indeed one wonders if there is not an aspect of the silly-clever in some of Louis Tiffany's art, beautiful though much of it is, and if his severer critics did not seize upon this party as exemplifying what they felt to be meretricious in his glass. At any rate the ball seems to have coincided with the beginning of the downgrading of his work, a process that was not to be reversed until after his death, which occurred in 1932. Surely it would have come as a surprise to the art world in the years of the Great Depression had it been told of the magnificent future display of Tiffany glass at the New-York Historical Society or of the prices now paid for his smallest pieces.

If the era of my concern coincides more or less with that of the sometimes-dubbed American Renaissance, what more appropriate key figure could it have than that jack-of-all-arts, Stanford White? For this large, commanding, genial, witty man of great goodwill, this scholar, eclectic collector, and splendid epicurean, was not only the master architect of his day; he was a painter, a sculptor, a water colorist, a designer and maker of jewelry and of sumptuous leather book bindings. He was in brief an American Cellini.

As one of his biographers, Charles C. Baldwin, has put it:

> To him everything in life—the paintings of Holbein, the cathedral of Laon, the shoulder muscles of Sharkey, Blanche Ring's singing, the wine at Martin's, the gilding on an old frame, salmon fishing, the cornice of the Maison Carrée, the voice of Emma Eames, the coffee at Delmonico's—was bully, wonderful, gorgeous. And he meant it. It was good to be alive in the eighties and nineties, to be allowed to hang turkey red curtains behind the windows of Fifth Avenue, to remake Madison Square with paper lanterns, to design eighteen-foot columns for the Astor balls, to decorate the Metropolitan Opera House with fifteen thousand roses, to plan club houses and churches, universities and apartment buildings.

But if White was one of the leaders who brought the Renaissance to America, it may be asked: Was it his own, or did he duplicate the Italian one? A young grandson of his is supposed to have commented, on a first visit to Florence: "But it's pure McKim, Meade and White!" And it is certainly true that White's greatest buildings suggest European models: the Century Club, a Verona palazzo; the University, that of the Strozzi. But whereas in the case of so much derivative architecture, including that of Richard Morris Hunt, the effect has a peculiar quality of dankness and heaviness, exuding an atmosphere faintly depressing to the observer, that of White is light and blithe—it seems to spring up from rather than to sit on its site. Does it really matter where an inspiration comes from if the conception and design are so fine? Would we care if we were to learn that the Parthenon had been modeled on a temple in Ephesus constructed three hundred years earlier?

White changed New York from a drab town of brownstone to a colorful cultural capital that evoked much of what was greatest in many civilizations. When accused of being derivative, he emphatically admitted the charge. Had not Rome plundered Greece? Every renaissance had its beginnings in the past—that was the meaning of a "rebirth."

White's charm, exuberance, and love of life made him a favorite in many circles of the New York social world. We meet him constantly in the published letters and memoirs of the time. Henry Adams, describing a circle of American friends in Paris in the summer of 1905, wrote, "The only truly serious person here is Stanford White, who is so mad that it doesn't matter." White's conversations, his parties, his trips abroad seem to blend with his work in a life that was a continuous and joyful pageant.

Of course, there were excesses. How could there not have been with such a man? He was not one to be confined to the compound of contemporary morals. His affair with the much younger actress, Evelyn Nesbit, need not have resulted in such disaster, or even come to the attention of the wife and son to whom he was utterly devoted, had it not been discovered, some time after its conclusion, by the brooding, neurotic Pittsburgh millionaire, Harry K. Thaw, whom Nesbit had subsequently succeeded in marrying. It was a strange and sordid example, on Thaw's part, of jealousy-after-the-fact, the subject so minutely studied by Proust throughout his great novel.

Thaw's savage murder of White in 1906 has played an unduly large role in the great architect's story. We tend to think of Marie Antoinette on the scaffold, of Nathan Hale with a rope around his neck, and of the unfortunate White at his table in the restaurant on top of his own Madison Square Garden as the fiend approaches him from behind. The case was made worse by the filthy lies that Nesbit told about White in court in an obvious effort to prejudice the jury and save Thaw's worthless life. It was the old case of putting the victim on trial instead of his assailant. But the notion that a man like White would use narcotics to seduce a woman is patently absurd. The epicurean in him alone, without assistance from the indubitable man of honor, would have rejected a drugged partner for the act of love. The indignation aroused in some portions of the public by the imagined picture of the wealthy quinquagenarian architect of the rich using nefarious tactics to overcome the "virtue" of a poor girl living alone in the wicked city reminds one of the almost contemporaneous fury evoked across the Atlantic by the trial of Oscar Wilde. There was surely a note of the philistine in it: "So *that's* what those artist fellows are really up to!"

White's commissions for the Vanderbilt family were numerous, but not among his best-remembered. Perhaps the finest one is the bronze doors of Saint Bartholomew's Church, given in memory of Cornelius II. The family preferred Hunt for their greater houses, as some of the Vanderbilt women preferred the fashionable portraitist Porter to the far greater Sargent. It may be just as well, as almost all of the larger New York private houses have been demolished. White's frequent presence on the city's streets and avenues still contributes significantly to the small amount of architectural feature and individuality we have left.

MRS. ASTOR
AND
WARD MCALLISTER

The William Astor family by Lucius Rossi.

WARD McALLISTER'S publication in 1890 of *Society as I Found It,* memoirs deemed fatuous even in an era not notably hostile to that quality, is supposed to have brought on his downfall as *arbiter elegantiarium* of New York society. But in truth that camel was already weary of its load of straws. Society had had its fill of playing the stately game of Windsor Castle with Mrs. Astor as the austere though far less mourning Queen Victoria; it was ready for Harry Lehr and Mamie Fish and parties with elephants and chimpanzees. To the eyes of the old guard this may have smacked of declining Rome; to our own, looking back, it is simply the change of sets in a musical comedy. "Mrs. Astor is an elderly woman," Mrs. Fish explained. And soon enough she would be one, too, and her "good old days" equally lamented.

Ward's credo contains many helpful hints to the would-be fashionable. If a thing is worth doing, it must be worth doing well, even if infinitives be split: "To properly frappé champagne, put in the pail small pieces of ice, then a layer of rock salt, alternating these layers until the tub is full. Put the bottle in the tub; be careful to keep the neck of the bottle free from the ice, for the quantity of wine in the neck of the bottle being small, it would be acted upon by the ice first. If possible, turn the bottle every five minutes. In twenty-five minutes from the time it is put in the tub, it should be in perfect condition, and should be served immediately."

Now this may be well enough for those with patience and fine palate; it is *cuisine,* and *cuisine* is international and indisputable. What appalls the reader of Ward's book is the complacency with which he reduces human conduct to the rules of *cuisine.* Good morals are simply good manners, and the devil himself no more than an uncouth social climber.

"If you want to be fashionable, be always in the company of fashionable people. As an old beau suggested to me, if you see a fossil of a man, shabbily dressed, relying solely on his pedigree, dating back to time immemorial, who has the aspirations of a duke and the fortune of a footman, do not cut him; it is better to cross the street and avoid meeting him."

Ward boasts, as one of the finest achievements of his earlier years, how he opened and refurbished a long unoccupied and shut-up family mansion in Madison, New Jersey, to have it ready for a ten-day house party of "a dozen of the most *difficile,* fastidious people of Newport":

Telegraphing at once to the agent who had charge of this house to put an army of scrubbing women in it, and have it cleaned from cellar to garret, I next went into the wholesale business of kerosene and lamps. . . . I hunted up an experienced chef, got my servants and then made menus for ten dinners, lunches and breakfasts; . . . engaged a country band of music for the evenings, telegraphed to Baltimore for my canvasbacks, arranged for my fish, vegetables and flowers to be sent up by train daily from New York; . . . looked after my stabling, and found we could stable twenty horses in a fine brick stable and house all the drags and vehicles.

Needless to say, his house party was the greatest success; his guests "lived for those ten days as thoroughly an English life as one would have lived in a country house in England." His only lapse in taste was to append this final sentence to the chapter he devoted to the great event: "This country party I gave in November, 1862." Was this to add further proof of the difficulties he had had to overcome? Surely, even as late as 1890, some of his readers were bound to contrast his achievement with Burnside's contemporaneous push into Virginia and its sad repulse at Fredericksburg. Perhaps the general had lacked Ward's resourcefulness.

Ward was born in 1827 in Savannah, of a New York mother and a Georgian father. The families of both were well-connected and well-to-do, but his father and older brother decided in the 1850s to take advantage of the discovery of gold in California and moved to San Francisco, whither Ward followed them to set up a law office. With the money rapidly earned there, plus the modest fortune of the woman he married (a muted, presumably patient character throughout his florid career), he was able to retire when still in his early thirties, travel widely in Europe, and settle at last in Newport, with a small townhouse in Manhattan, where he now embarked in all seriousness on his career as a social arbiter. Soon an expert in dress, food, wines, ball music, dancing, forms of address and invitations, and every nuance of etiquette, he proposed nothing less than to draw up a code of manners that would act as the constitution of upper-class social life in America.

For this he needed a chief of state, or a kind of sovereign, a personage whose wealth, lineage, and utter respectability would be beyond any challenge. The new rich, particularly the men, still smelling a bit from the heat of raw competition, were not going to submit docilely to a wine-sniffing, gloved and spatted dandy who, whatever courage he may have needed in his frontier life (and there must have been some), had by now concealed it behind a barrage of "my dear fellows" and "my charming ladies," prefacing his every emphatic assumption of his interlocutor's agreement with the elided "Dontcherno?" Indeed, only a woman could bring them into line. The tycoons themselves were too busy for the exacting tasks of society, and their male descendants too often preempted by sports or worse. Ward chose as the committee for his Patriarch Balls, which were to set new standards for the elect, twenty-five gentlemen with aristocratic qualifications, but for the supreme position he needed a lady, and he tells his reader in hushed tones how the choice was made, or rather how it providentially made itself.

The first Patriarch Balls were given in the winters of 1872 and 1873. At this period a great personage (representing a silent power that had always been recognized and felt in this community, so long as I remember, by not only fashionable people, but by the solid old quiet element as well) had daughters to introduce into society which brought her prominently forward and caused her at once to take a leading position. She possessed great administrative power, and it was soon put to good use and felt by society. I then, for the first time, was brought in contact with this *grande dame,* and at once recognized her ability, and felt that she would become society's leader, and that she was admirably qualified for the position. . . . With such a friend, we felt the Patriarchs had an additional social strength that would give them the solidity and lasting powers which they have shown they possess.

Caroline Schermerhorn, who had married William B. Astor, the grandson of John Jacob who had divided with his older brother the bulk of the family fortune, is not an easy character to put together. One keeps hoping to find her more interesting than she appears to have been. I remember once, on a two-hour drive with her grandson, Thornton Wilson, then in his seventies, suggesting that we kill the time by trying to re-create her personality. He jumped at the idea, for he had loved her and known her well and deplored "all the nonsense that was talked about her." He then, in all seriousness, proceeded to tell me every stale anecdote I had ever read in all the cheap books and magazine articles about the Four Hundred. I could only suppose that, as the image initially implanted on a tourist's retina of the Parthenon fades in time to be replaced by the memory of any old postcard or snapshot, so Thornton's own picture of a beloved grandmother had merged with all the banal legends. Perhaps the most vivid description that we have of Caroline Astor is that offered by Mrs. Winthrop Chanler (who married her husband's great-nephew) in *Roman Spring*: "Mrs. William B. Astor was the acknowledged leader [of New York society]. She always sat at the right of the host when she went to dinner parties; she wore a black wig and a great many jewels; she had pleasant cordial manners and unaffectedly enjoyed her undisputed position."

Plain, plump, placid, amiable, with temperate conventional principles and ideas, a good mother, an excellent housekeeper, always dignified, rarely ruffled, she would probably have been content to lead a quiet, unspectacular life had her husband wished to share one with her. But he didn't. She must have bored him, for he was always off on his yacht, leaving her and the children for months at a time. Why had he married her, this attractive and reputedly brilliant man, of intellectual tastes and vast fortune, who presumably could have had his pick of the beauties of old New York? We don't know. Her being a Schermerhorn was certainly an advantage, as had being a daughter of General John Armstrong been one for her mother-in-law. The Astors had no social ancestry beyond the first John Jacob. At any rate, it seems not to have been an asset to provide lasting attraction to a spouse who was never to find a motivating interest in his life and who turned to the high seas and the bottle.

Ward conveniently filled the vacuum that William had left.

Caroline was not a woman to take a lover; the wife now became all mother, and there were four daughters to launch. He played on her as Disraeli played on Queen Victoria; he dangled before her the romantic concept of becoming a queen. There is a John Leach cartoon that shows the wily prime minister as a turbaned swami tendering the imperial Indian crown to the austere, black-garbed but obviously tempted widow. Ward's proposal was an even harder one to resist, for it would give Caroline not only a social supremacy gratifying to a plain and neglected wife, but an occupation that would use all of her very considerable organizational abilities. She would provide the halls, the flowers (acres of them—she became known as the lady of roses), the sumptuous meals, the stately formal service. He would order the wines, arrange the cotillions and, above all, draw up and occasionally supplement the lists of the elect.

It worked. There is nothing like a team with perfect faith in the validity of what it is doing. New York society, made up largely of the wives, daughters, and daughters-in-law of financiers, industrialists, and their lawyers, and of their male heirs who had not been trained, like European désoeuvré aristocrats, to be elegantly or even usefully idle, was devoid of any true social function or purpose. The men did not go into public life, which was considered hopelessly corrupt and had been abandoned to the bosses, and the arts had not achieved the respectability as a career they had long enjoyed in the Old World. Ward's genius was to understand that what the more organized sex wanted it would get, and he offered the women a game of "court" that would give to the frivolity of extravagant entertaining some of the dignity of a governmental function. Passing before Caroline's "throne" in her ballroom, where she stood, diamond-studded, with her chosen "ladies" under her regal portrait by Carolus-Duran, one could at least fancy that one was paying obeisance to a popular sovereign.

Were people really that silly? Not all, of course. Some just wanted to dance. Some simply liked parties. Some went because it didn't occur to them not to. But I have learned to recognize certain kinds of smiles and jokes in social life that are intended precisely to deny what it would be ridiculous to admit: an inner reverence for wealth and grandeur. I am sure that many of Caroline's guests made fun of her pomposity and pretentiousness and smirked when they spoke of her with mock awe.

Yet if you take peoples' jokes literally, you are as often right as wrong. The man who grinningly says "I could kill my mother-in-law" may mean just that. And mock awe is often the masque of awe.

Caroline's parties were probably dull, but nobody minded that. The point was not to be amused; it was to be there. What is surprising is how long the game went on, with hardly any significant changes. Caroline, in late middle age, followed at last the lead of the Vanderbilts and commissioned their favored architect, Hunt, to build her one of the heaviest and most imposing of his French Renaissance châteaux on Fifth Avenue and Sixty-fifth Street, whither she moved from her more modest brownstone on Thirty-fourth, and the parties continued more grandly than ever. Ward died in 1895, but he had fulfilled his function; she needed him no more. People had begun to find him quaint and outmoded. There was a young man called Harry Lehr who was amusing people with his wit and impudence. Seeing Mrs. Astor enter a room, resplendent in diamonds, he told her that she looked like a chandelier. There was a pause. And then she smiled! She was amused. It was the beginning of a new era.

And the end of hers. Ward's truer instinct would have warned him that their system was one that could not afford raillery.

A few years before her death in 1908 Caroline's memory failed, and she retired from society. The great glass doors of the Fifth Avenue mansion, which were opened to an approaching visitor without his having to touch a bell, now remained closed. But a legend sprang up that discreet servants continued to go through the routine of announcing guests and pretending to pass dishes and pour wines at a long empty table at the end of which the witless old lady continued to talk left and right. Edith Wharton, whose father had been Caroline's first cousin, was inspired by these rumors to write one of her most vivid and chilling tales, "After Holbein."

Ward McAllister, despite his passion for what he called "nobs" and "swells," was not without an appreciative eye for men of greater force. He had learned something of these, perhaps, in his frontier days, and early in his New York career he had cultivated the acquaintance of old Commodore Vanderbilt. He relates in his memoirs how the magnate gave him a market tip:

A similar offer was made to me by my old friend, Commodore Vanderbilt, in his house on Washington Place. I was a great admirer of this grand old man, and he was very fond of me. He had taken me over his stables, and was then showing me his parlors and statuary, and kept all the time calling me "his boy." I turned to him and said: "Commodore, you will be as great a railroad king as you were once an ocean king, and as you call me your boy, why don't you make my fortune?" He thought for a moment, and then said, slapping me on the back: "Mc, sell everything you have and put it in Harlem stock; it is now twenty-four; you will make more money than you will know how to take care of." If I had followed his advice, I would now have been indeed a millionaire.

JOHN PIERPONT MORGAN

Entrance to the Pierpont Morgan Library, New York City,
designed by McKim, Mead and White and completed in 1906.

H E WAS the commanding figure of the era and would have been its fitting symbol had his standards not been so elevated. As it was, his concept of honesty and honor, buttressed by the immense power of his character, places him aside from his fellow financiers in a kind of gaudy golden niche of his own, a shrine from which emanate the rays of a personality that could strike the observer, depending on his light, as shrewd, arcane, stubborn, arrogant, idealistic, dramatic, megalomaniac, loving, suspicious, easily hurt, and naïve. I think the image he would have most liked to be remembered by is that of the massive and formidable old man, hunched over his game of solitaire in the great library gleaming with the treasures of the Renaissance, while from the antechamber the nervous captains of industry, summoned to avert the Panic of 1907, come in, one by one, each to propose his plan for saving the banks.

For where Morgan differed from other men of money was that they were concerned only with their own skins while he was concerned with his and theirs. He was passionately interested in creating an orderly and prosperous business community, and he had no doubt that capitalism was the only system in which this could be properly accomplished. But capitalists had to police themselves; a sound market had to depend on a gentleman's word. And one gentleman in particular had to take the lead, the only one with a long family tradition of honest banking and merchandising behind him, the son of Junius Morgan, partner of George Peabody, the great American banker of London.

As John Pierpont Morgan's bank in New York, a correspondent with his father's in England, grew in size and power in the final decades of the last century, it began to take control of the companies it reorganized in order better to sell their securities and to act as a peacemaker between them, persuading them that cooperation could be more profitable than price wars. When William Henry Vanderbilt's monopoly of railroads in New York threatened to turn the public and legislature dangerously against him, it was Morgan who planned the diversification of his portfolios. And it was Morgan who created those giant combinations, the Northern Securities Company and U.S. Steel. When Theodore Roosevelt remarked sarcastically that the great banker treated him as a peer, he was only describing literally the latter's attitude. Morgan not only believed he was the President's equal, but that he was a far greater influence for the public good. For was Roosevelt not using the Sherman Act to destroy his life's work? When the ex-President went on a safari to Africa, the organizer of trusts expressed the hope that the lions would do their duty.

There are some rare men, like Napoleon, who are big enough to shove history temporarily off the tracks. Morgan was not one of them. But if, as he testified to a congressional committee in 1912, four months before his death, American finance really *had* depended on a man's character, and if more businessmen had been possessed of his own, then indeed the Sherman Act and the New Deal, four decades later, might not have been needed. Morgan in the end could not do it all, even though his effort was a mighty one.

Today he is remembered as much for being a collector as a banker, and here too he set rather than followed the style. For he disdained the giant Hunt palaces of the Vanderbilts, filled with academic French and English art, preferring less ostentatious yet still roomy and comfortable country houses and city brownstones and cramming them with beautiful works of art from different civilizations for the delectation of his family and friends. It may even have been a kind of reverse snobbishness that made him build a fishing shack in Newport. But his social instinct was sure. He would have cut a smaller figure had he mingled with the Four Hundred in the ballrooms of Fifth and Bellevue avenues. On Madison Avenue and Thirty-sixth Street, on the Hudson or, best of all, on board his yacht, the *Corsair,* he reigned supreme.

His collection, or rather collections, for he purchased the lifetime accumulations of others, dated from 1890 when his father's death vastly increased his resources. He started with literary manuscripts, but he soon expanded his field enough to justify his wife's comment:

"Pierpont will buy anything from a pyramid to a tooth of Mary Magdalene." A reliquary for the latter is now in the Metropolitan Museum.

The thirty-five huge crates in which the London collection was transported to New York in 1912, after the high duties on art had been repealed, contained jewels; porcelains; reliquaries; eucharistic vessels; biblical scenes carved in ivory, boxwood, or rock crystal; Chinese screens; Egyptian sculptures, miniatures of European royalty and nobles; gold medallions; gold and onyx snuff boxes . . . well, there was no end to it.

Can we derive a clue as to what sort of things he most preferred in that mammoth pile? We can certainly deduce that he loved glittering, elaborately wrought pieces that had once been the baubles of monarchs; that he may have tried to reconcile his own religious faith with his greed for showy objects in the very splendor of his liturgical vessels and ecclesiastical paintings; and that, when it came to portraits, he preferred, as he did with friends, subjects that were young and beautiful. It may be worth pointing out that his passion for surrounding himself with lovely things and people increased in the last half of his life in seemingly direct proportion to the acne that so cruelly disfigured his nose and face and surely contributed to his shyness and to the brusqueness of his manners.

How good was his taste? It is hard to tell in a man who bought whole collections, who was willing to purchase a vitrine of *objets de virtu* to obtain a single piece. But nothing sharpens the eye like expensive mistakes, and Morgan was a skilled merchant who was heavily engaged in the purchase of art for a quarter of a century. Certainly the quality of his things now in the Metropolitan Museum and the Morgan Library is of the highest, and to duplicate the entire collection that he left in 1913 might break a bank in Tokyo.

Such a man, however, always attracts detractors, and certainly Roger Fry was the greatest of these. The English art critic came to the Metropolitan Museum as curator of European paintings late in Morgan's life. Morgan entirely dominated his fellow trustees, and it was sometimes difficult to tell when he was buying in the interests of his own collection and when for the institution. Fry, acting as his adviser in a summer in Italy in 1907, seems to have been serving Morgan in both capacities and detesting him in both.

He relates how Morgan became intrigued by a large seventeenth-century crucifix, not in itself a remarkable work of art, when the dealer showed him a concealed stiletto that could be whipped out of the shaft of the cross. "Shows what the fellows did in those days!" Morgan exclaimed. "Stick a man while he was praying! Yes, very interesting."

Fry's comment on the incident, often quoted in books on Morgan, is sufficiently devastating: "For a crude historical imagination was the only flaw in his otherwise perfect insensibility."

But to Fry, herald of the Post-Impressionist school, the dominating presence of a man who could afford to buy all the beautiful things he wanted to buy, without anything like the keenness of Fry's vision, and who lacked the smallest interest in any of the wonderful canvases that were being painted in his own day, must have been galling indeed. It should also be pointed out that Fry described the incident *after* he had been dismissed from his post at the Metropolitan at Morgan's insistence in a dispute over a painting that Fry wished to buy for the museum and that Morgan wanted for his own collection.

There is no first-class biography of Morgan. For that we must wait for Jean Strouse, the author of an excellent life of Alice James, who is devoting years to a study in depth of the banker-collector. Until then I find *J. Pierpont Morgan, an Intimate Biography,* by Herbert Satterlee, his son-in-law, the best source of illumination. It has long been discounted as a work of hagiography; Satterlee's reverence was such that he was even supposed to have sought Morgan's permission before accepting an appointment as assistant secretary of the navy. But if one knows how to read discreet memoirs in the Victorian tradition, one can benefit from the author's undoubted intimacy with his subject and at the same time make out many things that are carefully (too carefully) glossed over.

Although in a less reverent era it has been easy enough to smile at Morgan's passion for attending the triennial conventions of the Episcopal Church as a lay delegate and arriving at them in a private railroad car filled with bishops, his faith all his life was simple and deep, even glimpsed through the florid prose of his son-in-law: "The practice of hymn singing he kept up in his own home after he married. From his boyhood there were certain hymns of which he was fond, and he loved to sing them over and over again. As he grew older these hymns were associated with many of the happiest evenings of his life. And as an elderly man he sang them just as vigorously as he had done when he was a youngster, but with deeper feeling, and sometimes when one of them was finished he would sit looking into the fire for several minutes without moving."

And there is no mistaking the sincerity of this letter of Morgan to his wife describing a visit to the Church of the Holy Sepulcher in Jerusalem in 1882:

The whole thing was so different, so entirely different, from what I had preconceived that I can hardly yet realize that I have really been on a spot which has been held for so many centuries to be sacred. . . . Turning to your left, you ascend stairs, and you find yourself in a vaulted chapel, built upon what is supposed to be the summit of Calvary; a death-like stillness pervades, the distant sounds of an organ in a distant part of the church are heard; awestruck and impressed you stand almost breathless upon what must always be the most sacred spot on earth. I cannot attempt to describe my feelings; words fail me entirely. I could only say to myself: it is good to be here. . . . Impelled by an impulse impossible to resist you fall on your knees before that shrine.

Morgan's limitations as a collector are distinctly, if unintentionally, set forth by his son-in-law, according to whom:

He had no use at all for the pictures of Impressionists, for "modern" music or for writers who dealt with morbid themes or social problems. Attempts at modernity or realism in those lines were absolutely distasteful to him. His spiritual faith was like the Rock of Gibraltar, and his adherence to tenets of clearly wholesome art and literature was always one of his strongest characteristics. In the great library which he left, there was no erotic literature. It was always weeded out from the collections which he bought and in the notable collection of pictures which he made there were none that he could not exhibit as fine examples of their type. Everything that he did showed clean healthy tastes and habits.

Satterlee's own knowledge of literature, at least in French fiction, must have been decidedly inferior to his father-in-law's, for he goes on to record that among the manuscripts in this nonerotic collection was that of *Nana,* with which Morgan refused to part, even when Zola's widow tried to repurchase it.

And as for the banker's much-rumored marital infidelities, what more does one need than Satterlee's description of the *Oceanic* incident? When Mrs. Morgan sailed to New York in 1899 on the maiden trip of the White Star liner *Oceanic,* her husband came out to meet her in quarantine on the *Corsair*. As soon as the health officer's visit was concluded, Morgan resolved to board the liner to greet her, and Satterlee relates what followed:

A launch shot under *Corsair*'s stern and came over to *Oceanic*. The passengers crowding the rail watched the doctor go down the rope ladder . . . drop on to his little tug and go off. Immediately the *Corsair* launch came up to the ladder. I saw that the Commodore [Morgan] was the only man in her besides her crew. Word ran around the decks of the *Oceanic* that Mr. Morgan was coming on board, and necks were craned over rails and heads came out of portholes to see him. The tide was swirling by the big ship. He grasped the lower end of the rope ladder, swung up on it and his launch disappeared in the direction of the

Mr. Morgan's private study (c. 1910) in the Morgan Library.
Above the mantlepiece, a portrait of Junius S. Morgan;
on the walls, a virtual pantheon of Renaissance painting
by Raphael and his school.

yacht. The ladder swayed with his weight against the ship's side which was rough with overlapping plates and innumerable bolts. In Mr. Morgan's mouth was a cigar. He looked up once, then fixed his straw hat more firmly on his head, and with his teeth clenched on the cigar, he started up. It was a climb over sixty feet straight up to the rail. To everybody who was watching him it was quite evidently a foolhardy thing for him to attempt. The sight of the swirling water below was enough to make a person dizzy, and he was climbing an up-and-down ladder to a point higher than the cornice of an ordinary four-story dwelling house. I knew that he was sixty-two years old, weighed 210 pounds, and never took any exercise, and it seemed to me that his progress was very slow, although he never stopped and came steadily upward. Some of those on the yacht turned away, too frightened to watch him. The time was long enough for the sporting element on the decks of *Oceanic* to make bets as to whether he would ever reach the rail. If he should fall, there was very little chance of doing anything for him in that tideway. When his face, dripping with perspiration, appeared over the rail, and he got where he could throw his leg over it, he waved aside all the outstretched hands and asked: "Where is Mrs. Morgan?"

Even had I never heard the rumors of Morgan's lady friends, this gesture would have struck me as the bravado of a husband who had something on his conscience. And the discreet Satterlee does not help matters by the assertion that Mrs. John B. Markoe was included on yachting expeditions because of her skill at dominoes.

But most interesting of all is Satterlee's assertion that all of his father-in-law's friends were "of gentle birth and good breeding." This way of classifying people today excites derision, but to Morgan and his family it was a very serious thing. It came down again to what the great banker said at the congressional investigation of 1912, that the only factor that really mattered to him in making a loan was the character of the applicant. He was determined that the world in which he lived, even if he had to remake it, would be an honest one, and then it would deserve to be the recipient of all the treasures that he had culled from ancient civilizations. If the task was beyond him, and if the era in the end could be more truly labeled a Vanderbilt one than a Morgan, it was not for any lack of effort on his part.

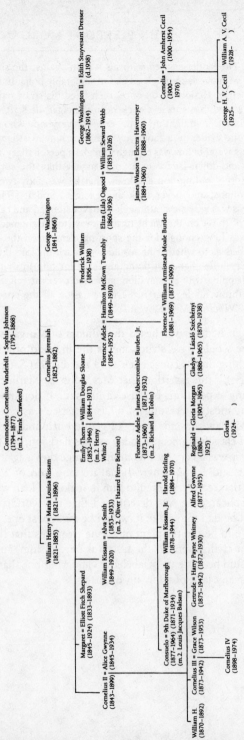

Genealogical Chart of the Vanderbilt Family (Only those persons treated in the text appear)

INDEX

INDEX

INDEX

ABOUT THE AUTHOR

Louis Auchincloss is the author of over forty books—novels, biographies, and collections of short stories and essays—including *The Rector of Justin, Diary of a Yuppie,* and *Fellow Passengers.* He lives in New York City with his wife, Adele, a descendent of Commodore Vanderbilt.